To Radio Mumbler,

Best wishes

Pat Williams

One Hundred Years

of the

GOWER SHOW

by Pat Williams

Published by
The Gower Agricultural Society

Copyright © The Gower Agricultural Society

Published in 2006 by
The Gower Agricultural Society
in association with
Llanrhidian History Group
c/o Big House, Llanrhidian
Swansea, SA3 1ER

A CIP catalogue record for this book is
available from the British Library.

ISBN 0-9547450-2-7
978 0 9547450 2 8

Printed and bound in Wales by
Dinefwr Press Ltd.
Rawlings Road, Llandybie
Carmarthenshire, SA18 3YD

Cover photograph:
The Centennial Show
(By kind permission of Stephen Thomas, Tal-y-Ffrawe)

Contents

The Centennial Show. Photograph by Gayle Marsh.
(By kind permission of the South Wales Evening Post).

Memories

A hundred years ago, the Gower folk you know
Decided that they'd like a village fete.
So some did undergo, to start the Gower Show
In the castle grounds of the estate.

The Show in Penrice Park, was a great thing to embark,
And people travelled far to rendezvous.
So for twenty years or so, this fledgling Gower Show,
Did alternate between there and Kilvrough.

It was a great day out, for the locals there's no doubt
A chance to meet and talk to friends and neighbours.
To see how well they'd done, if prizes they had won,
And celebrate the fruits of all their labours.

There were classes for lambs, and prize-winning rams,
Shire horses and small mountain ponies.
There were cattle and roots, and flowers and fruits,
Home cooking and cockerels and conies.

We watched the show grow, and the Park overflow,
And a Fairwood move was essential.
So the Show said goodbye, with a tear in its eye,
To a site which was full of potential.

But it went with a frown, 'twas too close to the town,
They say bigger is not always best.
And there was a remark, to move home to the Park
And the Show in itself was redressed.

It was very well planned, with some local trade stands,
A food hall, a craft tent and honey.
A place for growing crops, a marquee serving hops,
'Midst the laughter and jingle of money.

A country show again, in its usual domain,
A place to have a picnic in the shade
With a view of Oxwich Bay, then off without delay
Around the ring to watch the Grand Parade.

And so we celebrate, this very special date
That started o'er a hundred years ago.
We hope that this will be, a great centenary
For our super rural country Gower Show.

John Beynon

CHAPTER 1

The Early Years of the Gower Show

An early photograph of the Gower Show.
(By kind permission of V. Jones, Lunnon).

Two shows were held in Gower during the 1890s – the Gower Christmas
Fat Stock Show and Penrice Flower Show. The Fat Stock Show, held in a
field adjoining the King Arthur Hotel, was comprised of cattle, pigs,
poultry, grain and roots. A number of animals were sold later in the day
there at auction through the 'persuasive eloquence of Mr. F. F. Meager'.

The last Fat Stock Show took place in December 1905, and its president Admiral Lyons and secretary Mr. Arthur Anthony then became
leading officials of the Gower Agricultural Society.

Penrice Flower Show was founded in 1891, and, in addition to floral
displays, had classes for vegetables, fruit and poultry. Sheepdog trials
were also held, and proved a great attraction.

In 1902, David Ace of Llangennith was presented with a silver medal at the Penrice Flower Show that had been donated by E. Parsons & Co., Seedsmen, Swansea. David Ace, a tailor, lived in the Post Office in Llangennith.

Silver medal presented to David Ace, at the Penrice Flower Show, 1902.

(By kind permission of John Beynon, the great-great-grandnephew of David Ace).

Port Eynon celebrated the success of one of its parishioners in the Flower Show in the Gower Church magazine of 1903. It recorded that Captain Hopkins, who besides winning thirty other prizes, had won 'the chief prize for the best and neatest garden in the Peninsula!' It noted that Captain Hopkins was 82!

The 1903 Flower Show had 1,400 entries, and the performance of Llanelli's Town Band 'was a delight to everyone'.

Schedule of 1914 Flower Show.
(By kind permission of Barrie Jones).

Over **£130** in *Prizes*.

Rules and Schedule of Prizes of the 24th

WEST GOWER

Horticultural Show

of Cottage Garden, Dairy and Poultry Produce,
to be held (by kind permission of MISS TALBOT) in

PENRICE PARK,

On Thursday, August 13th, 1914.

Entries close August 4th, 1914,

All Entries to be accompanied by Entrance Fees where stipulated, otherwise the Entries will not be accepted.

GEO. JENKINS, Bull Croft, Oxwich, Reynoldston.

QUOITS.

For the Best Four Quoits (Open). 1st prize, 10/-, given by Mr. A. Anthony; 2nd, 5/-, given by Mr Mansel Bevan; 3rd 2/6, given by the Hon. Sec. Entrance Fee 6d.

Entries close 4th August, 1914.

Quoits competition.
(By kind permission of Barrie Jones).

Quoits were a popular pastime in Gower until the 1930s, and most villages had their own team and a quoit bed. A quoits competition was held in the 1914 flower show, with a first prize of 10/- offered for the 4 best quoits.

LLANRHIDIAN QUOITS TEAM, 1912.
Back row from left – Mr. Cross, Arthur Williams, Harry Thomas, Stan Brockie, George Edwards, E. Jenkins and Charles Tucker. Middle row – John Dunn, A. Rees, Bert Dunn, Frank Jones and Mr. James, schoolmaster. Front – T. Jones, George Thomas, Jack Thomas and Will Jones.
(By kind permission of Mrs. N. Payne).

The Flower Show continued at Penrice Park until 1914. No shows were held during the war years and it was amalgamated with the Gower Agricultural Show in 1919.

GOWER AGRICULTURAL SHOW

Will be held NEAR

Penrice Castle. Reynoldston.

(By kind permission of Miss Talbot)

THURSDAY, SEPTEMBER 20th, 1906.

GRAND EXHIBITION OF
CATTLE, HORSES, SHEEP, PIGS,
CORN AND ROOT CROPS.
JUMPING, TROTTING, AND TURN-
OUTS.

Upwards of 500 Entries. Judging at 11 a.m.
A LUNCHEON will be provided on the
ground at 1.30 p.m. by Mr. J. E. Pitt,
Grand Hotel, Swansea. Tickets—2s. each.
General Refreshments at Popular Prices.

A. ANTHONY. Hon. Sec.

1779

Advertisement of the First Gower Show.

THE FIRST GOWER SHOW

The first Gower Show was held on Thursday, 20th September 1906. An advertisement in the *South Wales Daily Post* on the 18th September 1906 publicised the event, and listed amongst the attractions 'A luncheon will be provided on the ground at 1.30 p.m. by Mr. J. E. Pitt, Grand Hotel, Swansea.'

An extensive account of the show in the *South Wales Daily Post* on the 20th September noted that 'as a yearling it did exceedingly well,' and paid tribute to Miss Talbot for putting a large field on her Penrice Castle grounds at the commit-

GOWER'S NEW VENTURE.

AGRICULTURAL SOCIETY'S FIRST
SHOW.

GOOD ENTRIES AND GATE.

1906 report in the S   th Wales Daily Post.

tee's disposal, adding that 'a more delightful spot could have not been chosen.'

The report recorded that the Secretary Mr. Anthony received 480 entries, and the stamp of the exhibits was 'in a word – eighteen carat!'

The Glamorgan County Council Agricultural Committee offered prizes in the dairy section, which was open to those who had at any time attended the County Council Travelling Dairy School. In the horse section was a class for colliery horses, open to the best mare or gelding not exceeding 15 hands, suitable for underground colliery purposes.

Amongst the agricultural firms represented on the field were Messrs. Weaver, Swansea, who had a tent with samples of their feeding cake on show.

Weaver & Co., Swansea.
(By kind permission of Mrs. B. Dunn).

Special prize-winners included D. Harry, Cillibion, for Best bull; J. S. Brockie, Park – best tenant's cow or heifer and best agricultural brood mare (cup given by Society) – Mansel Bevan, Overton.

David Harry of Cillibion (left) with his prize-winning bull.
(By kind permission of Mrs. Thelma Pritchard).

Miss Emily Talbot, 1840-1918.
(By kind permission of Thomas Methuen Campbell).

Miss Talbot inherited the Penrice and Margam estates on the death of her father C. R. M. Talbot in 1890. Her obituary in the Gower Church magazine of October 1918 recorded that 'she loved Penrice where she had spent a great deal of her happy childhood, and always looked forward to the autumn months which she would spend at the Castle.' It went on to recall her generosity in restoring many Gower Churches and her numerous contributions to charitable institutions.

The parish of Pennard noted in the Gower Church magazine of 1906, that Admiral Lyons, who was the President of the Show, had won two firsts, a special and a second with 'a very good sow'.

The show then alternated each year between Penrice and Kilvrough.

On the 7th September 1907, the Gower Agricultural Society had met at the Jeffreys Arms Hotel in Swansea two weeks before the 1907 show, for the purpose of approving the list of

GOWER FARMERS

Meet in Force at the Jeffreys Arms Hotel.

South Wales Daily Post.

show judges. The Secretary, Mr. Anthony, was instructed to buy a cup of the value of £2.2s to be given by the Society as a prize at the show for the best pen of sheep.

The parish of Ilston recorded in its 1907 entry in the Church magazine that 'the show had been held in glorious weather and amidst delightful surroundings in a field at Kilvrough.'

Pennard farmers were well represented at the 1907 show, and won prizes with their cattle, horses and sheep. Mrs. Griffiths, Highway, who had also won prizes in the first Gower Show, secured five prizes, including one for butter making.

The Gower Church magazine recorded that the 1908 show 'favoured with glorious weather, was again held in Penrice.' In Port Eynon's entry, Mr. Francis Clement of Monksland, who, for three years in succession had won 'Captain Bostock's

Penrice Show, 1908.

Bullin's Brake – Gower Show
Return Fare 2s.6d.

cup for the best pen of breeding ewes', was awarded the cup in perpetuity; Rhossili listed 12 prize-winners, and at Llandewi, Messrs. James won 1st prize and a Silver Cup given by R. Helme, Hillend, for a shorthorn bull in the Tenant Farmers' Class.

The 1909 Show at Kilvrough, which was advertised in the Gower Church magazine, 'noted with satisfaction' that Lady Lyons had consented to be President, and announced that prizes offered by the Society would amount to over £150.

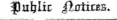

Public Notices.

GOWER AGRICULTURAL SOCIETY.

President—LADY LYONS.

GREAT SHOW
AT
PENRICE CASTLE,
REYNOLDSTON

(by kind permission of Miss Talbot) on
THURSDAY, SEPTEMBER 15, 1910.
300 Entries for Horses, Cattle, Sheep, Pigs,
Corn and Root Crops, Turn-outs, Trotting
and Jumping Competitions.
Show open at 9.30 a.m. Judging at 11
o'clock sharp. Admission, 1s.
Luncheons, Teas and General Refreshments.
Caterer—Mr. J. E. Fitt.
Motor Omnibuses will leave Jeffreys
Arms Hotel, and Brewery Tap Hotel,
Swansea, at frequent intervals.
A. ANTHONY, Hon. Sec.
Penrice Castle Estate Office, Reynoldston.
6202

Tuesday, 13th September 1910.
Advertisement for the
Gower Show in the *Daily Post*.

Lady Lyons.
(By kind permission of V. Jones, Lunnon).

The fifth annual show, held at Penrice on the 15th September 1910, saw a very large number present. The 746 entries included 75 cattle, 170 horses, 92 pens of sheep and pigs. In a 'Special' class, was a class for a mare or gelding suitable for Yeomanry.

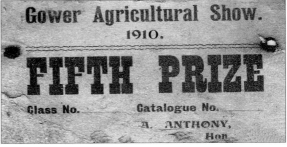

Fifth Prize card awarded at the 1910
Gower Show to H. Jones, Lunnon.
(By kind permission of V. Jones, Lunnon).

The sixth Gower Show was held on the 14th September 1911, and an entry by Llandewi parish in the Gower Church magazine congratulated the Messrs. Clement of Scurlage Castle on their success – for the third time in succession they won the Challenge Cup, value £10.10s.0d. for their brood mare. Messrs. James of Llandewi had won second prize for their bull in the tenant farmers' class and Mr. Stanley Jones of Knelston had gained a first prize for his pen of crossbred ewes.

A day at Penrice
Castle Park, 1912.

First prize card awarded to H. Jones, Lunnon,
at the 1912 Gower Show.
(By kind permission of V. Jones).

18th September 1913.

Great Show at Penrice Castle,
17th September 1914.
(By kind permission of Barrie Jones).

A 1914 1st prize-winning ram
for Messrs. Gordon Bros.,
Tyle House Farm,
Burry Green.

*(By kind permission of Mr. Deane
Gordon).*

No shows were held during
the First World War, and the 1919
Gower Show was heralded as
'Gower's Peace Show with fine
exhibits at Kilvrough.'

GOWER'S PEACE SHOW

Fine Exhibits at Kilvrough.

The parish of Ilston recorded in the Church magazine that the show
was noticeable for the large number of prizes gained by the Home Farm,
Kilvrough, and the remarkably good attendance of visitors, the gate
money being double as much in any former year.

Gower Show Winner, *The Herald of Wales*, 27th September 1919.
'One of the first prize winners at the Gower Agricultural Show
on Thursday at Kilvrough, a fine Hereford bull owned by
Mr. F. Ffitch Mason of The Faraam, Killay.'

CHAPTER 2

Through the Twenties and Thirties

GOWER AGRICULTURAL SHOW

AT

PENRICE CASTLE,

On Thursday, Sept. 16, 1920.

Nearly £300 in Prizes for Cattle, Horses, Sheep,
Pigs, Goats, Dairy Produce, Corn and Root Crops.
Saddle, Driving, and Trotting Classes.
Open Horse Shoeing Competition.

Penrice Estate Office,
Reynoldston.

Entries close 30th August to
A. ANTHONY, Hon. Secretary.

(Advertisement from the Gower Church magazine).

Admiral Heneage-Vivian, Vice-President of the Gower Show in the 1920s.
(By kind permission of Peter Naylor).

A prize-winning bull, owned by T. E. Jenkins, Kilvrough Farm,
shown by his stockman, Charles E. Williams, Big House Farm, Lunnon.
(By kind permission of John Williams, Big House Farm, Lunnon).

Three generations of the Jenkins family, Kilvrough Farm.
From left – Rowland Jenkins senior, Rowland Jenkins and T. E. Jenkins.
T. E. Jenkins and his son Rowland Jenkins both served
as secretaries of the Gower Agricultural Society.
(By kind permission of Martyn Jenkins).

Gower Agricultural Society.

President : Major The Lord Blythswood, M.V.O.

GREAT SHOW AT PENRICE CASTLE,

On Thursday, August 17th, 1922.

Over £300 in Prizes.

Poultry and Vegetables added to Prize List.

Schedules and Entry Forms may be had on application to :—
Hon. Secretary, Penrice Estate Office, Reynoldston.

(Gower Church magazine).

GOWER'S GREAT SHOW.

President ... ... MAJOR THE LORD BLYTHSWOOD, M.V.O.
Vice-President ... ADMIRAL A. W. HENEAGE-VIVIAN, C.B., M.V.O.

14th ANNUAL SHOW

On KILVROUGH FARM,

PARKMILL,

(by kind permission of T. E. JENKINS, Esq.) on

Thursday, August 16th, 1923.

Over £300 in Prizes.

Live Stock ; Saddle, Harness and Trotting Classes,
Horse Shoeing & Timbering Competitions.
Poultry, Vegetables, Fruit, Honey, and Dairy
Produce Classes.   Corn (in Sheaves) Roots.

Schedules and Entry Forms now ready and may be
had on application to Hon. Secretary, Mr. A. Anthony,
Penrice Estate Office, Reynoldston.

Entries positively close on Monday 30th July, 1923.

(Gower Church magazine).

In 1924, Lt. Col. Ernest Helme D.S.O. of Llangennith organised a Gower Pageant in aid of the Gower Nursing Association. It was to be held at Penrice Castle on the 14th August 1924. Each village enacted a traditional Gower episode, including St. Madoc's Mapsant by Llanmadoc and Cheriton, and an 18th century smuggling scene by Rhossili. The villagers spent many hours making the costumes and rehearsing their scenes. Although the pageant was a great success, it rained torrentially all day, so it was decided to re-enact the pageant at the 1924 Gower Show.

On the 4th September 1924, the pageant was performed, this time in fine weather.

The parish of Penmaen noted in the Gower Church magazine: 'we had a magnificent day for the Gower Show, with the added attraction of a repetition of the Gower Pageant and were able to enjoy a fine day for the second performance.'

Avis Marshall (née Gordon) took part in the scene performed by Port Eynon and Horton parishes. They re-enacted a 14th century Bidding Wedding.

Thomas W. Gordon, the officiating priest at the Bidding Wedding, with his wife Elizabeth, who was a wedding guest. Daughter Avis and son Eddy were village children.
(By kind permission of Mrs. Avis Marshall).

Four generations of the Taylor family, Overton, took part in the Bidding Wedding scene at the Gower pageant.

From left – Albert Taylor, The Bower, Port Eynon – the Fiddler; Fred Taylor, Great House, Horton – the bride's brother; Ernest Stevens, The Bays Farm, Overton – a wedding guest and George Taylor, Croft House, was a 'holder of the rope'.
Centre – Irene Stevens, bridesmaid. Front – May and Molly Grove, children.
(By kind permission of Dennis Cooke).

'Trotting Maid' 7693, with Mr. John Harry, Llethryd, a silver medal winner at the 1924 Gower Show.

(By kind permission of Mrs. Phyllis Davies).

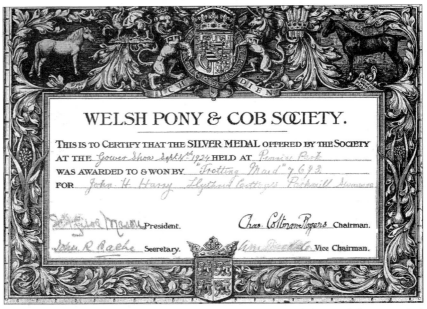

1924 Certificate confirming that the Silver Medal of the Welsh Pony and Cob Society was presented at the Gower Show 1924 to 'Trotting Maid', a cob belonging to Mr. John Harry, Llethryd.

(By kind permission of Mrs. Phyllis Davies).

The Arrangements Book for the 1925 Gower Show includes cost of hiring marquees, accommodation for judges, and requirements for the shoeing competition.

(By kind permission of the Gower Agricultural Society).

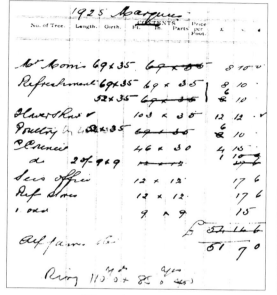

Hire of marquees.   Shoeing requisites.

(James' Marquees by kind permission of Barrie Jones).

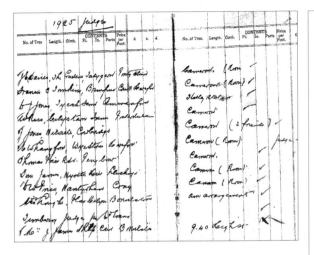

Accommodation for judges at the
Hotel Cameron.
(By kind permission of Mrs .B. Dunn).

OFFICIALS OF THE GOWER SHOW, CIRCA 1925.
Included here are – centre back row, Hopkin Ll. Prichard, with his white horse.
Front row from left – Arthur Anthony, 3rd left – T. E. Jenkins, Kilvrough,
4th left – F. Fitch Mason, 5th left – C. C. Vivian.
(By kind permission of Martyn Jenkins).

The 1925 show was the last to be held at Kilvrough Farm. From this date, the show was held annually at Penrice.

FASHION AT THE GOWER SHOW, 1920s

Standing – Florrie Lucas and Mary Jeffreys.
In front – Ann Bennett and Elizabeth Ann Dark.
The four friends, all from Gower, were in service locally and the Gower Show was a day's holiday for them.
(By kind permission of Dr. Beryl Apsitis).

GOWER SHOW OFFICIALS, 11th SEPTEMBER 1926
Standing – Messrs. W. R. Prosser, Judge, T. E. Jenkins, J. Stanley Pike, Vet. Surgeon, C.C. Vivian, Treasurer, A. Anthony Sec., W. R. Board, Judge.
Seated – Mr. Claude Thompson, Admiral Heneage-Vivian, Vice-President, Lord Blythswood, President, Messrs. W. A. Jenkins, Percy Rowlands and A.O. Thomas.
(By kind permission of Martyn Jenkins).

Lord Blythswood's Advice.

Winners of the Farm Competitions.

The official luncheon was presided over by Lord Blythswood, who was supported by Admiral Heneage-Vivian, Mr. Claude D. Thompson (chairman of the Agricultural Committee), and officials.

The toast of the "Agricultural Society" was given by Mr. Thompson, who remarked upon the fact that the Gower Agricultural Society was going along on sound business lines. They were out to produce the best possible article.

Lord Blythswood, in responding, deplored the national disregard for the agricultural industry, and offered some advice on the necessity for breeding good cattle strains in Gower. "Breed the best, it always pays," he said, for whatever the vicissitudes of the country, the best stock always finds the best market.

His lordship also commented upon the winners of the farm competitions, and announced the results as follows:—

1. Mr. Hy. Jones' farm, Lunnon, Parkmill; 2, Mr. Mansel Bevan's farm at Overton; 3, Mr. Morgan Davies' farm, Killay.

Admiral Heneage-Vivian proposed the toast of the "Judges," and Mr. W. P. Davies, Pontypridd, responded, after which Archdeacon Williams proposed a vote of thanks to Lord Blythswood.

GOWER AGRICULTURAL SOCIETY,
2nd SEPTEMBER 1926
This cup was presented to
Mr. Henry Jones, Lunnon in 1926
by W. A. Jenkins Esq., Swansea,
for the best conditioned and
cultivated farm in Gower. Mr. Henry
Jones won the cup on three separate
occasions, and this entitled him to
keep it in perpetuity.
(By kind permission of Mr. Ernest Jones).

Daily Post records Lord Blythswood's advice, September 1926. He announced that the winner of the cup for the best conditioned and cultivated farm in Gower was Mr. Henry Jones, Lunnon.

Mr. Henry Jones, Lunnon (centre), 1926, with a prize-winning steer.
(By kind permission of Dr. J. Jones).

Corn mows at Lunnon Farm, winner of the best-cultivated farm in Gower.
(By kind permission of Mr. Emrys Jones).

GOWER SHOW OFFICIALS, 1927
(*South Wales Daily Post*)
Seated from left – Admiral Heneage-Vivian, Lady Blythswood,
Lord Blythswood (President), the Hon. Mrs. Methuen, the Mayor of Swansea,
Councillor D. J. Bassett and Mr. A. Anthony (Show Secretary).
Included in the back row are – Mr. A. Thomas, Mr. H. Ll. Prichard,
the Hon. L. Methuen, Councillor W. A. Thomas and Mr. C. C. Vivian (Treasurer).
(By kind permission of the Gower Agricultural Society).

The Gower Show remembered . . .

NANCY PAYNE (NÉE DUNN) OF PENGWERN FARM

I remember going to the Gower Show in the 1920s, when I was just four years old. I walked with my parents from Pengwern to Cillibion and then over Cefn Bryn to Penrice. When we arrived we went to see the butter-churning competition, where my mother's friend Lily Davies of Leason Farm was competing. She was dressed all in white, and her head was covered with a white scarf.

In those days there was always a dance in Reynoldston Hall on the evening of the Show.

MRS. GWEN BEYNON,
FORMERLY OF WESTERNSIDE FARM, HORTON

My father George Tucker was a tenant farmer of Westernside Farm, Horton, which was part of the Penrice Estate then owned by Miss Emily Talbot. I would visit Mr. Anthony, the secretary of the estate, in his cottage in Reynoldston to pay the rent on the farm. My father was on the Gower Show committee in the early years, and would often call on Mr. Anthony in his horse and trap to discuss the arrangements for the Gower Show.

We had two traps – the Sunday trap and the everyday trap. On Gower Show day, we would take our corn and vegetables to the show in the everyday trap. We would have stripped the corn and bound it up ready for the judging. The vegetables – swedes and mangolds – would have been washed and then we would travel from Horton to the Show. I was one of seven children, so as soon as we arrived we would be off to see the sights. We always knew so many people there! My father, as a committee member, would take luncheon in a marquee with Lady Blythswood and the other dignitaries, but my mother would have to look after us all.

To raise money for the show, each village had its own collector. They were given a book in which to record the contributions that had been made. My father was given a book for Horton and I went around Horton for many years collecting from the villagers. There were often visitors who would come to stay at Horton every summer, and they would also make contributions. Mr. Anthony was always so pleased that I had collected so much money.

The South Wales Transport Co., Ltd.

= 𝔖how =

AT

PENRICE CASTLE PARK,

Reynoldston, September, 6, 1928

Augmented Service of Motor
Omnibuses will be run by this
Company in connection with
the above Show.

RETURN
FARE : **2/3** from .
SWANSEA

TRADE STANDS.

Messrs. Leonard Smith & Co., Causeway
Mills, Blackheath, Birmingham.
The Polienta Co., Oxford Street, Reading.
Gartons Ltd., Seedsmen, Warrington.
Messrs. F. Hewthorn & Co., Ltd., 7-15
Lamb's Passage, Chiswell Street,
E.C.1.
Messrs. B. C. Tipper & Son, Ltd., Birming-
ham.
The Briton Ferry Chemical & Manure Co.,
Ltd., Briton Ferry
The Glamorgan Beekeepers Association
Beekeeping Appliances
Messrs Furneaux & Thomas, Opposite
Victoria Station, Swansea
Kohler Automatic Electric Light Plant.

(Gower Church magazine).

GOWER'S GREAT SHOW.

Splendid Exhibits In The Penrice Grounds.

A GOWER WINNER.

Daily Post, 7th September 1928.
'Dawn' owned by Mr. H. Crawford,
Killay, ridden by Miss Barbara Brook,
1st prize-winner in the ladies
hackney class at the Gower Show.

Headline news in the *Daily Post,* 1929.

(By kind permission of Ellis Davies).

David Morgan at the Gower Show, circa 1920s.
(By kind permission of Robert Davies, Knelston).

JOHN MORGAN, REYNOLDSTON – my father, David Morgan, founded his Reynoldston stores in 1916. He was an agent for Lister products and a general agricultural merchant to the Gower farmers.

ARTHUR ANTHONY, LAST OFFICIAL AGENT TO THE PENRICE ESTATE AND GOWER SHOW SECRETARY, REMEMBERED BY JOHN MORGAN, REYNOLDSTON

(By kind permission of the Gower Agricultural Society).

In the early part of the 20th century, Arthur Anthony, a Llanelli man, applied for the vacant position as an assistant to the Agent, Mr. H. Ll. Prichard, and was successful.

To reach the Estate Office in Penrice, every Monday he would catch a train at 6 a.m. from Llanelli G.W.R. station to Gowerton, and then change to the L.M.S. station to take him to Llanmorlais. From here he had to walk up over the Bryn, across Welsh Moor Common and through Black Lane to Cillibion. He would then walk along the Red Road (as

33

it was known in the 1930s) towards Reynoldston. When he reached Holywell he would turn left and join Hayeswood Lane to the Home Farm, and cross the main road to the Estate Office.

He would work here all day, then walk to his lodgings at King Arthur Cottage, Reynoldston. Mrs. Bidder occupied this cottage. Arthur Anthony would carry two suitcases all the way – one with clean clothes and the other with food. (Food was rationed during the 1st World War.) He did the reverse journey every Friday afternoon. This he did for several years until he married Miss A. Williams, also from Llanelli. They then settled at Hayes Cottage, Little Reynoldston.

After the death of Mr. Prichard, Mr. Sinnett was appointed Agent, but stayed only a few years when Mr. Anthony filled his post. Shortly afterwards, most of the farms owned by the Estate were sold – the tenants were offered first refusal. John D. Woods and Co., London, handled the sale. Their local representative was Mr. Reynolds; he was a very fair person.

Mr. Anthony was the secretary of the Gower Show Agricultural Show for many years for which he was greatly respected. He remained both Estate Agent and Show Secretary until his death in 1951.

THE GREATEST ONE-DAY SHOW IN WEST WALES.

GOWER AGRICULTURAL SOCIETY.

President ... ... THE LADY BLYTHSWOOD.
Vice-Presidents ... ADMIRAL A. W. HENEAGE-VIVIAN, C.B., M.V.O., D.L.
F. FFITCH MASON, Esq.; H. LL. PRICHARD, Esq., J.P.; C. C. VIVIAN, Esq., J.P.

TWENTY-FIRST

GREAT SHOW

AT

Penrice Castle Park,

(by kind permission of the LADY BLYTHSWOOD) on

Thursday, September 4, 1930.

Over £400 in Prizes. 12 Challenge Cups. 220 Classes.

Riding. Driving, Jumping, Musical Chairs.
Horse Shoeing Competition.
Sheep Dog Trials, commencing at 12 noon.
Poultry (Utility) and Rabbits. Garden Produce. Honey.
GREAT FLORAL EXHIBITION.
Exhibits and Demonstrations by the Glamorgan Federation of Women's Institutes.
Show open at 10 a.m. Judging punctually at 11 o'clock.

Refreshment of all kinds on the Grounds.
Reduced Return Fares on all the Omnibus Routes.
Entries definitely close on 18th August.
Schedules now ready, and may be obtained from Mr. G. Jenkins, Woodside, Oxwich, or from Hon. Sec., Mr. A. Anthony, Penrice Estate Office, Reynoldston.

(Gower Church magazine).

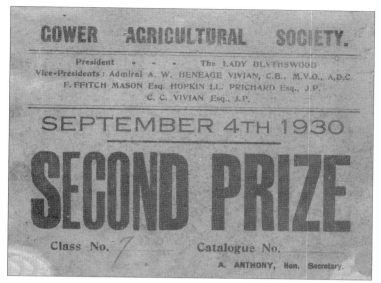

GOWER AGRICULTURAL SOCIETY.

President - - - The LADY BLYTHSWOOD
Vice-Presidents : Admiral A. W. HENEAGE VIVIAN, C.B., M.V.O., A.D.C.
F. FFITCH MASON Esq. HOPKIN LL. PRICHARD Esq., J.P.
C. C. VIVIAN Esq., J.P.

SEPTEMBER 4TH 1930

SECOND PRIZE

Class No. 7   Catalogue No.

A. ANTHONY, Hon. Secretary.

Second Prize card awarded to H. Jones, Lunnon,
at the 1930 Gower Show.
(By kind permission of V. Jones, Lunnon).

This steer, owned by Messrs. Gordon of Tyle House Farm, Burry Green,
won three 1st prizes at the 1930 Gower Show.
(By kind permission of Mr. Deane Gordon).

GOWER SHOW, CIRCA 1930s

A 1st prize-winning bull from Berry Farm
with Arthur Tucker, Phyllis Tucker and Billy Bowen.
(By kind permission of Ernest Smith, Oxwich).

A prize-winning bull from Old Henllys with, from left – Arthur Tucker,
Rees Tucker, J. Harry, Gwyn Williams, Tom Long, Andrew Thomas,
Lake, G. Beynon and M. Richards.
(By kind permission of Ernest Smith, Oxwich).

GOWER AGRICULTURAL SOCIETY.

Dr.   Income and Expenditure Account for Year ended 31st December, 1931.   Cr.

EXPENDITURE.	£ s. d.	£ s. d.	INCOME.	£ s. d.	£ s. d.
To Prizes		370 18 0	By Subscriptions		285 0 6
Judges		19 3 4	Donations		68 2 6
Hire of Marquees ...	33 10 0		Show Receipts—		
Hire of Poultry Pens ...	8 17 4		Entrance Fees	60 12 1	
Hire of Chairs ...	3 3 4		Admission	190 12 9	
Hire of Public Address Equipment	6 6 0		Car Park ...	34 16 0	
		46 16 8	Sheep Dog Trials Enclosure ...	4 19 0	
Ground Expenses including labour, haulag.&c	70 13 9		Catalogues	20 2 3	
Police		8 17 6	Catering Rights	25 0 0	
Printing, Stationery, Advertising, etc. ...		118 2 5			336 2 1
Postages, Telegrams, etc.		29 3 2	Dividends on Investments—		
Clerical Assistance		4 14 6	5% War Stock 1929-47—Gross	5 0 0	
Insurance		4 1 6	4½% G.W.R. Stock—Net ...	6 19 6	
Show Secretaries' Association		0 10 6			11 19 6
Cheque Books, etc.		2 8 6	Bank Interest		2 1 3
Official Luncheon		28 19 8	Income Tax refunded ...		3 0 9
Depreciation of Hurdles		12 0 0	Miscellaneous Income ...		1 0 0
			Balance, being excess of Expenditure over Income, carried to Balance Sheet		9 2 11
		£716 9 6			£716 9 6

Balance Sheet as at 31st December, 1931.

	£ s. d.	£ s. d.		£ s. d.	£ s. d.	£ s. d.
CREDITORS		25 0 0	INVESTMENTS—At Cost—			
INCOME AND EXPENDITURE ACCOUNT—			£100 5% War Stock 1929-47 ...	102 11 0		
Balance at Credit thereof, per last Balance Sheet	614 4 2		£200 4½% Great Western and West Cornwall Railways Rent Charge Stock ...	200 0 0	302 11 0	
Deduct—			(Note—The market value at the above date was £261)			
Honoraria to Hon. Secretary and Assistant for 1930 Show ...	63 0 0		HURDLES—At Cost, less amounts written off, per last Balance Sheet	23 2 8		
	551 4 2		Add—Purchases during the Year to date	11 10 0		
Deduct—				34 12 8		
Excess of Expenditure over Income for the Year to date, per attached Account	9 2 11		Deduct—Amount written off in respect of depreciation, per attached Account	12 0 0		
		542 1 3			22 12 8	
			SUBSCRIPTIONS—Outstanding ...		15 0 0	
			CASH—At Bankers	218 12 1		
			In hands of Hon. Secretary	8 5 6	226 17 7	
		£567 1 3			£567 1 3	

AUDITOR'S REPORT.—I have compared the above Balance Sheet and the attached Income and Expenditure Account with the relative Books, Accounts and Vouchers, and find them to be properly drawn up in accordance therewith. I have obtained confirmation from the Bankers of the balance in their hands and I have verified the Investments as at the date of the Balance Sheet.

2nd February, 1932.   P. O. WILLIAMS, Chartered Accountant, Auditor, Swansea.

PLATE PRIZES.   Holders 1931/32.

	Holders 1931/32.
The Faraam Challenge Cup for Farms over 50 acres	In Hand
The Hamilton W. Crawford Cup for Farms under 50 acres	In Hand
The Faraam Challenge Cup for Hereford Cattle	Tucker Bros, Old Henllis
The C. C. Vivian Challenge Cup for Shorthorn Cattle	D. Beynon, Ponthenry
The Clyne Cup for Dairy Cows	Tudor Radcliffe, Margam
The Kilvrough Challenge Cup for Heavy Horses	J. Richards, Bynea
The Faraam Challenge Cup for Mountain Ponies	Elias Williams, Morriston
The T. E. Jenkins Cup for Jumping	T. G. Jenks, Rumney
The Society's Cup for Poultry	A. Jenkins, Sketty
The Clyne Cottage Gardens Cup...	A. Hoyles, Fforestfach
Thorley's Special for Cattle	R. T. Board, Bridgend
Hadfield's Special for Mangolds	H. V. Watters, Porteynon
Hadfield's Special for Swedes	1st—H. V. Watters, Porteynon 2nd—T. Bevan, Dunvant
The Edmund G. Bevan Cup, Horticultural Section	A. Johnston, Swansea

Balance sheet for 1931.

(By kind permission of Ernest Smith, Oxwich).

LADY BLYTHSWOOD ACCOMPANIED BY COMMITTEE MEMBERS

From left – Councillor Arthur Griffiths (Chairman of Committee), C. C. Vivian Esq. J.P. (Hon. Treasurer), Arthur Anthony (Hon. Secretary), Lady Blythswood (President), the Hon. Olive Methuen-Campbell, and Hopkin Ll. Prichard J.P.

(By kind permission of Mrs. Dorothy Tucker).

```
                    GOWER AGRICULTURAL SOCIETY.


                           AGENDA.
                      20th February 1932.

1.   To read and confirm Minutes of last Annual Meeting.

2.   To receive Report and Statement of Accounts for the
     year ending 31st December 1931.

3.   To fix site for 1932 Show.

4.   To fix date for 1932 Show.                Retiring officials
                                               eligible for re-election.
5.   To elect officers:

          1.   President.                      The Lady Blythswood.

          2.   Vice-Presidents.                Mrs. F. Ffitch Mason.
                                               Mr. H.Ll.Prichard. J.P.
                                               Mr. C.C.Vivian.J.P.

          3.   Chairman of Committee.          Mr. Arthur Griffiths.

          4.   Vice-Chairman of Committee.     Mr. Kenneth Jenkins.

          5.   Hon. Auditor.                   Mr. P. O. Williams
                                               Chartered Accountant.

          6.   Hon. Veterinary Surgeon.        Mr. J.S.Pike,M.R.C.V.S.

          7.   Hon. Treasurer.                 Mr. C.C.Vivian, J.P.

          8.   Two members to sign cheques.    Mr. H.Ll.Prichard.J.P.
                                               Mr. C.C.Vivian, J.P.

          9.   Hon. Secretary.                 Mr. A. Anthony.

         10.   Assistant Secretary.            Mr. G. Jenkins.

         11.   Executive Committee.

         12.   Committee to revise Prize List.

         13.   General Purposes Committee to   Chairman, Vice-Chairman,
               deal with objections etc.       Messrs H.Ll.Prichard,
                                               W.A.Jenkins,J.P.,
                                               T.E.Jenkins,Mansel Bevan,
                                               A.W.Griffiths,Richd.Beynon,
                                               A.O.Thomas,  J.Thomas.

6.   Revision of Rules (if necessary).

7.   Votes of thanks.

8.   Any other business.
```

Agenda for meeting on the 20th February 1932.

(By kind permission of Ernest Smith, Oxwich).

THE SOCIAL SIDE OF THE GOWER SHOW, 1932
(Daily Post)

Standing from left – Mr. A. E. Griffiths, Mr. D. R. Grenfell M.P., Mr. H. Ll.
Prichard (behind in trilby), Mr. J. K. Jenkins (Chairman), Ven. Archdeacon
Harold Williams, C. C. Vivian J.P., Mr. Stanley Pike, Mr. Lewis Jones M.P.,
Mervyn Davies (Brecon NFU Chairman), Mr. Arthur Thomas J.P.,
Sec. A. Anthony, Mr. Lewis (Welsh Rep. F.U.), Mr. W. A. Jenkins J.P.,
and Mr. D. W. Richards (Swansea Labour Exchange).
Seated from left – Mrs. Lewis Jones, Lady Blythswoood, T. Byng Morris,
and Lady Leighton (Lady Blythswood's sister).
(By kind permission of the Gower Agricultural Society).

Daily Post, September 1932.
'Keen Rocket', owned by D. Thomas
of Penmaen, won several prizes
at the 1932 Gower Show.

Evening Post –
'Mr. Joe Brayley of the All Whites
holds a first prize-winning
colt "Blossom".'

'A fine jump over hurdles by one of the competitors
in the Jumping Classes at the Gower Show'.
(*Herald of Wales, 3rd September 1932*).

LLANRHIDIAN W.I. AT THE GOWER SHOW

EILEEN HUTIN

My mother, Mrs. Violet Morgan of Sunnyside, Llanrhidian, was a founder member of Llanrhidian W.I. when it was formed in 1919. I well remember her buying loganberries and raspberries from Esther Harry who lived 'under the hill' in Llanrhidian, in order to bottle the fruit in Kilner jars to compete in the W.I. section of the Gower Show. She did gooseberries the same way too.

She would sit by the table, her glasses on the end of her nose, and, with a skewer, she would place each piece of fruit in the jar, just like a builder building a brick wall. She had such patience, and enjoyed it so much. She won many prizes over the years for her preserves, for her bottled fruit, chutneys and pickles. The shelves in her pantry were a treat to look at.

Gower Show Day was a 'must', and my father would drive us over to Penrice early in the morning, in order for her to place her entries in the W.I. tent. It was all very exciting, and we loved the day out.

In 1932, all the members of Llanrhidian W.I. helped to weave a rug which was later raffled with the proud announcement – 'A woollen rug, value £7.7s.0d which won first prize at the Gower Show.

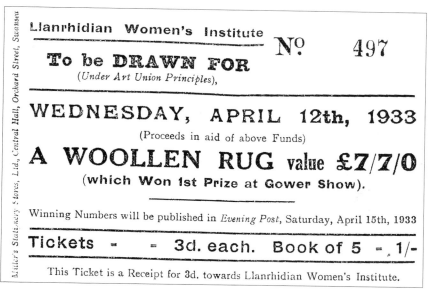

Llanrhidian Women's Institute
N⁰ 497

To be DRAWN FOR
(Under Art Union Principles),

WEDNESDAY, APRIL 12th, 1933
(Proceeds in aid of above Funds)

A WOOLLEN RUG value £7/7/0
(which Won 1st Prize at Gower Show).

Winning Numbers will be published in *Evening Post*, Saturday, April 15th, 1933

Tickets = = 3d. each. Book of 5 = 1/-

This Ticket is a Receipt for 3d. towards Llanrhidian Women's Institute.

Miller's Stationery Stores, Ltd., Central Hall, Orchard Street, Swansea

Raffle ticket.
(By kind permission of Mrs. E. Hughes).

The Gower Show was a great attraction to the children in the Gower Schools. As it was always held on Thursdays, there was a great deal of absenteeism – as noted in the logbook for Llanmadoc School on the 1st September 1932:

'Attendance very low today, owing to the Annual Agricultural Show taking place in Penrice.'

By the time of the following year's show, the school had accepted the inevitable and recorded:

'Friday, 7th September 1933. Half-holiday granted for the Annual Agricultural Show at Reynoldston.'

THE GREATEST ONE DAY SHOW IN WEST WALES.

GOWER AGRICULTURAL SOCIETY.

President ... ... THE LADY BLYTHSWOOD.

Vice-Presidents ... F. FYITCH-MASON, Esq., H. L. PRICHARD, Esq., J.P., C. C. VIVIAN, Esq., J.P.
The Hon. LAURENCE P. METHUEN.

TWENTY-FOURTH

GREAT SHOW

will be held in the beautiful Grounds of

Penrice Castle, Reynoldston,

(by kind permission of the President) on

THURSDAY, SEPTEMBER 7th, 1933.

Over £400 in Prizes.   14 Challenge Cups.   220 Classes.

Wonderful Exhibition of Cattle, Horses, Sheep, Pigs, Poultry, Rabbits, Corn, Roots,
Garden Produce, Dairy Produce, Honey.

Riding, Handy Hunters, Musical Rides & Leaping Competitions. SHEEP DOG TRIALS.

GREAT FLORAL EXHIBITION.

Exhibits & Demonstrations by Members of the Glamorgan Federation of Women's Institutes.

Show open at 9.30 a.m.   Judging at 10.45 a.m.

PUBLIC LUNCHEON at 1.15 p.m.   Refreshments of all kinds on the Ground.

Special service of Motor Omnibuses to and from the Show from all parts.

Parties of 12 and upwards may obtain admission tickets at reduced rates provided application is made
to the Secretary not later than Saturday, Sept. 2nd, 1933.   Entries close August 21st, 1933.

Schedules now ready and obtainable from Mr. G. Jenkins, Woodside, Oxwich, or
Hon. Secretary, A. Anthony, Penrice Estate Office, Reynoldston.

Special Evening Entertainment, commencing about 5.30.

Champion Solo Competition—First Prize £4/4/- & Cup.

Exhibition of Folk Dancing by Gower School Children.

COMMUNITY SINGING supported by well-known Choirs.

Organized by the "Evening Post."

Castle Grounds Flood Lighted by The South Wales Electric Power Co.

(Gower Church magazine).

Herald of Wales, September 1933.
Old Penrice Ruins took on a strange beauty when they were
floodlit for the Gower Show.

42

MRS. GWYNETH JONES, LUNNON FARM

When I was in Three Crosses, Junior School, I remember that we were chosen to perform folk dances at the evening entertainment in the Gower Show in 1933. We had red and green ribbons to wave, as we belonged to the Urdd. The stage was in front of the castle at Penrice, which was floodlit. It all looked very spectacular.

Gower Show, 1933.
(By kind permission of Mrs. Margaret Davies, Knelston).

The sheepdog trials, Gower Show, 1933.
(By kind permission of Mrs. Ivy Griffiths, Llanrhidian).

1934 *Daily Post*. 'See the best of the west in Gower's Greatest Show'. Enterprising firms that contribute to the Show's success.

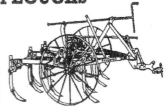

AUSTIN VANS

WE ARE EXHIBITING AT
THE GOWER SHOW

A full range of Austin Vans and the New Austin 10cwt. Truck. SPECIAL VAN DISPLAY at our new Show-rooms until August 31st. — UNION STREET

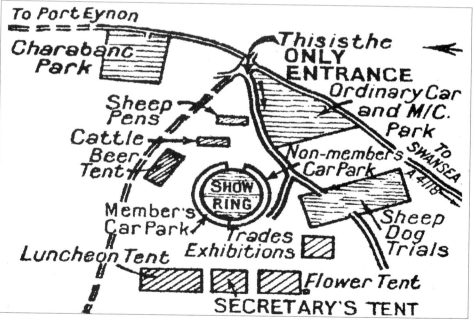

Map of the Showground, 1930s.
(By kind permission of Keith Evans).

Round the Ring at the Gower Show, circa 1930s.
(By kind permission of the Gower Agricultural Society).

GOWER SHOW, 1935

Martin Jenkins, Hen Parc Lane, at the Gower Show, 1935.
(By kind permission of Mrs. M. Alexander).

46

Martin Jenkins, Hen Parc Lane, far right, at the 1935 Gower Show.
(By kind permission of Mrs. M. Alexander).

GOWER SHOW DAY IN THE 1930s REMEMBERED
BY MARGARET ALEXANDER, HEN PARC LANE, KILLAY

When I was young, my father Martin Jenkins bred Welsh Mountain Ponies, and the Gower Show was always the highlight of the Gower year for us as a family. My father would show in the horse section, my brother Geoff entered his bantams, we would both enter the wild flower section, and my mother entered the cookery classes, so, as you can imagine, life was rather hectic in our house when we were getting ready for the show.

My mother Letty made up an outsized hamper to take to the show – a large joint of ham was cooked, also a fruitcake and a few large sponge cakes. Filling up the hamper was a large dish of butter, two loaves of bread, tomatoes from the greenhouse, and salad items, together with a very large carving knife. My mother and I had to walk up the lane to the bus stop, which was quite a long way, so by the time we arrived there the hamper seemed very heavy.

The evening before the show was always very exciting with all the preparations! My job, apart from getting the flowers ready, was to whiten the bridles, reins and the two pairs of shoes for my father and brother to

The Jenkins family, Hen Parc Lane, at the 1935 Gower Show.
(By kind permission of Mrs. Margaret Alexander).

run with the horses. I duly whitened everything and put it all on the hedge outside our cottage to dry. Later in the evening, my brother went to bring them in – but his shoes were missing! They were never seen again. Earlier, we had seen a tramp go past, so we decided that he must have taken them. He must have thought it was his lucky day, and no doubt he looked very smart in his glowing white shoes!

When my mother and I arrived at the show, we would make our way to the top of the field near the ring, where we would meet up with my Dad and brother who had gone down earlier with the horsebox. After setting out a tablecloth on the ground, she would be all set! I would take off to wander around the show, meeting one and all. Cousins, friends, and friends of friends would ask me where my mother was; after I had directed them they would be off! They always knew there would be a feast awaiting them! My aunt Gladys and family would come from Burry Port to join us, bringing a large box of Welsh cakes, and although it was like 'feeding the 5,000', I don't remember my mother ever running out of food.

They were wonderful times and a real social event, meeting so many people that we knew, and hadn't seen since the previous show. It was always a really lovely day – and even more special when we won. One year, my Dad won the Lord Swansea trophy – I think it was the first time that it was presented at the show. He was so proud and thrilled that he, a Gower man, had won it.

My Dad died in 1944, so the show never had the same place in our hearts after that – though we always went every year.

The Jenkins family, Hen Parc Lane, share a family picnic at the Gower Show.
(By kind permission of Mrs. Margaret Alexander).

South Wales Evening Post, 2nd September 1936.
'A great show in a glorious setting'.

GOWER SHOW, 1936

Three firsts and 4 seconds. Lenny and Elvet Jeffreys, Crickton Farm.
(By kind permission of Dr. Beryl Apsitis).

REACHING THE SHOW FIELD

In the early days, there were few lorries in Gower, and the competitors would have to walk their animals to Penrice or Kilvrough.

At Lunnon Farm, the farm workers would walk with the cows and bull through the lanes to Penrice. Ernest Jones remembers that his grandparents, Henry and Mary Jones, would go in the trap. His grandmother would use the leppanstock (stone mounting block) outside the farm to climb into the trap. He recalled that in the 1930s, his uncle Ivor Jones had taken a bull to the Show, which had won first prize. Unfortunately, it then went berserk, and caused much alarm amongst the onlookers. It was eventually loaded into a lorry and taken straight to the slaughterhouse. At the end of the show it was announced, with great satisfaction, that the bull had been shot!

Emrys Francis of Wernffrwd remembers going to the show with Will Richards of Hendy Farm, Penclawdd, in the 1930s. They travelled across Cefn Bryn in a horse and trap. Will would take his dog along to compete in the Sheepdog trials. They parked their horse and trap, with many others, in the lane opposite the entrance to the field.

Dick Beynon, Llanrhidian, recalls the care that would be taken by the Jeffreys of Crickton to get their horses to Penrice. 'The horses that we would take to the show were working horses, so it wasn't until they had finished their day's work that we could start preparing them for the show. We would groom them, and early next morning we would plait their manes, and then set off for Penrice. There was an old roadway leading from Crickton to the red road that led over Cefn Bryn. We would lead the horses over the pathway, taking care not to cross gutters where they could get muddy. We headed up towards Talbot's Road, and then down to Home Farm at Penrice. Most of the local farmers would walk their animals to the show – there were very few lorries in those days!'

Deane Gordon of Tyle House Farm, Burry Green, remembers the days when the show was held alternately at Penrice and Kilvrough. 'My father Hubert Gordon of Tyle House Farm would walk his cattle, ewes and lambs to the show, the rams would be taken in the trap and my

Dick Beynon, Llanrhidian, carried this photograph with him throughout the Second World War to remind him of home. For security reasons, he had to remove the words 'Gower Show'.
From left – Dick Beynon, Lenny Jeffreys, Elvet Jeffreys.
(By kind permission of Dick Beynon, Llanrhidian).

51

father would cover the top with netting. On Show day, there would be small groups of men and animals walking towards Penrice or Kilvrough from all the Gower villages. From Tyle House Farm we would walk from Burry Green to Llethryd and then down through the "Cwms" to the show field.'

Gower Show, 1936, two firsts and 2 seconds.
From left – Arthur Tucker, Peter Meyrick and Morgan Tucker.
(By kind permission of Milwyn Layton).

From left – Lady Blythswood, Mr. H. Ll. Prichard, Major F. Morgan, Messrs. T. Gibbons, W. A. Jenkins, T. Harris, A. O. Thomas, J. S. Jenkins and A. Anthony.
(By kind permission of the Gower Agricultural Society).

POULTRY TRUSSING AND DRESSING REMEMBERED BY DORA JONES, LLANRHIDIAN, A COMPETITOR IN MANY SHOWS

I have always loved chickens! I used to work for the Dunn family at Parc y Rhedyn Farm, and every Friday was feathering day. We used to prepare the birds for market on Saturday, and I learned how to dress them properly. I used to enter the poultry trussing class at the Gower Show. It was very competitive! There were different weight classes – and you had to get the bird to exactly the right weight. I used to spend hours the night before the show preparing them. I would even trim the gizzard to get it to the right weight – and if I cut off too much I would go and kill another hen and start again!

In one show I won a first, second and third, and I said to my husband Leonard, "That's it! I can't do better than that!" and that was the last show I entered.

GOWER SHOW, 1937

Mr. Arthur Evans, Pitt Farm, Penrice, with his shire horse 'Fairy', which won 1st and 2nd prizes at the 1937 Gower Show.
(By kind permission of Mrs. Olwen Evans).

Preparing the cattle for the show ring, 1930s.
(By kind permission of the Gower Agricultural Society).

The show ring, 1930s.
(By kind permission of the Gower Agricultural Society).

A TRIP TO THE GOWER SHOW IN THE 1930s REMEMBERED BY JOAN BEYNON, EASTERN SLADE FARM, OXWICH

I was born in Swansea, but spent all my summer holidays with my grandparents at Eastern Slade Farm in Oxwich. I loved to come down to Gower, and the highlight of the holidays was a trip to the Gower Show. My grandparents would hire Arthur Smith from Oxwich, and he would drive us to the Show in his car. There were few cars in Gower in those days so I was very excited to be travelling to the Show in such luxury!

JOHN WILLIAMS OF COURTHOUSE, ILSTON REMEMBERED BY KATHLEEN WILLIAMS, BIG HOUSE FARM, LUNNON

My uncle, John Williams of Courthouse, Ilston, used to attend many shows – including the Gower Show – where he would show his poultry. He always took a homing pigeon with him, and if he had won a prize, he would send the bird off home with the good news, so that his family would be the first to know!

Rowland Jenkins, Gower Show, 1937.
(By kind permission of Martyn Jenkins).

Rowland Jenkins, with Gloria and John Davies at the 1937 Gower Show.
(By kind permission of Mrs. Gloria MacLeod).

Gloria and John Davies, grandchildren of
Capt. Leighton Davies, at the 1937 Gower Show.
(By kind permission of Mrs. Gloria MacLeod).

John Davies, left, on his pony 'Gallant', and Gloria Davies, right,
on her pony 'Snowflake', at the 1937 Gower Show.
(By kind permission of Mrs. Gloria MacLeod).

FRANCES CHELEY (NÉE WILLIAMS),
FORMERLY OF COURTHOUSE FARM, ILSTON

My earliest recollections of the Gower Show were when, at a very young
age, I would visit my best friend Joan Evans (later Thatcher), who used
to live in The Towers. My mother would put me on the bus at 'The White
House' – in the charge of the bus conductor – and Joan would be waiting for me at The Towers. Joan had a sister Irene who used to work at
Penrice Castle, so we would walk down through the Park to the Show.

There were sideshows there, and I well remember the Hoopla stall,
run by Lady Blythswood. Joan and I had a go – and unfortunately when
I threw a hoop I broke a vase. I was told that I would have to pay for it,
but became so upset it was treated as an accident.

Years later, when I had children on my own – Daphne, Elizabeth and
Barrie – I encouraged them to participate in the Gower Show, by entering the Schoolchildren's section. One class was a bunch of wild flowers
to be shown in a 2lb. jam jar, and another class was a collection of wild
flowers to be named separately, and shown in 6 1lb. jam jars. Prizes were
won, and their interest grew through the years, and now the girls have
careers in floristry.

Although I have now retired, I was a very keen competitor myself, with success taking me far afield. The Gower Show has given us as a family so much pleasure. Now my great grandchildren are taking part, and I am sure that they will have as much fun and pleasure in the future shows as we did – and still continue to do!

The Leading West Wales Show.

GOWER AGRICULTURAL SOCIETY.

PRESIDENT   THE RIGHT HON. EVELYN LADY BLYTHSWOOD, PENRICE CASTLE.

VICE-PRESIDENTS--

F. FFITCH MASON, ESQ., H. LL. PRITCHARD, ESQ., J.P., C. C. VIVIAN, ESQ., J.P.
THE HON. LAURENCE F. METHUEN.

Hon. Secretary:
A. ANTHONY.
(TELEPHONE: REYNOLDSTON 21)
PRIVATE ADDRESS

Hon. Treasurer:
C. C. VIVIAN, ESQ., J.P.

Bankers:
MIDLAND BANK LIMITED.,
SWANSEA.

Penrice Castle Estate Office,
Reynoldston, Glam.

29th October, 193 7

Dear Sir (or Madam),

     You are requested to attend a Special Meeting of the above Society at the Valley Hotel, Bishopston, on Friday next, the 5th November, at 7.30 p.m., when the Hon. Mrs. Douglas, the donor, will present the Lord Swansea Trophy to the owner of the winning pony at the recent Show.

     The opportunity will also be taken by the Rt. Hon. Evelyn Lady Blythswood, who will preside, to present the unclaimed cups to any winners who may attend.

     Subscribing members of the Cefn Bryn and Fairwood Pony Associations are cordially invited.

     Light refreshments will be generously provided by the Hon. Mrs. Douglas.

                Yours faithfully,

                    A. ANTHONY.
                      Hon. Secretary.

(By kind permission of Ernest Smith, Oxwich).

THE GOWER SHOW REMEMBERED BY AUBREY OLIVER, FORMERLY OF SLADE FARM, OXWICH

As a young boy, for me the main attraction at the Gower Show was a horse belonging to Mr. Harry Thomas who kept the Tivoli Cinema in Gowerton. 'Harry Tiv', as he was known, would take his horse to all the local shows and challenge anyone to ride it. There would be a prize of £5 for anyone who could stay on its back for a certain amount of time – and of course, we all thought we could win it. But the horse was virtually impossible to ride. It would do anything to get you off – roll over – throw its head – and I never succeeded in winning the prize money.

I only know of two people from Gower who ever did. One was Will Tucker of Rhossili, and the other was Brynmor Grove from Hennyswell.

At the end of the show, Harry would climb onto the horse's back, and, quiet as a lamb, the horse would head for home.

'King Cole', owned by Major Ronald, Pennard, is shown here by Harold Williams, Llanrhidian at a 1930s Gower Show.
(By kind permission of John Williams, Lunnon).

For many Gower children, their first experience of competing in the Gower Show would have been in the wild flower section.

SCHOOLBOY MEMORIES OF DONALD LEWIS, FORMERLY OF WEOBLEY CASTLE

I remember as a schoolboy before the last war, collecting and identifying wild flowers, which in those days were plentiful.

I then decided to enter the children's class for wild flowers in the Gower Show. On the Sunday before the Show – which was on the first Thursday in September – we went in my father's car to Oxwich to get some of the rarer plants like sea holly, teasels and great mullien. I was able to identify a large number of the flowers through collecting cigarette cards, as there was one series of 50 on wild flowers. Most of a school-

1938 advertisement in the Gower Church magazine.

GOWER SHOW, 1939

From left - ?, ?, William Taylor, Elias Taylor, George Taylor (Parker Stores – tractor owner), Reg Jenkins, Gwyn Lewis, Cyril Nicholas.
Seated is George Nicholas.
(By kind permission of Randolph Jenkins, Llanmadoc).

boy's general knowledge in those days came from these cards. We were always asking smokers, 'Please could I have the card?'

When Show Day arrived you had to exhibit six named varieties, and a jar of mixed flowers and grasses. The named varieties were in jam pots, and the mixed varieties in a stoneware jar. After the judging I learnt that I had gained second prize, but the judge told me that if, instead of arranging the flowers in the large jar in an attractive arrangement as I had done, I had filled it to overflowing with more flowers, I would have won first prize. But I was still the proud recipient of 4 shillings!

THE GOWER SHOW, 1939, REMEMBERED BY ERIC MORGAN, FORMERLY OF LLANRHIDIAN

I remember that although the German army entered Poland on the day after the 1939 Gower Show, there seemed to be little thought or talk of war, perhaps because we had been assured of 'peace in our time'. I recall

GOWER SHOW,

THURSDAY, 31st AUGUST, 1939.

SPECIAL ENGAGEMENT OF

THE BAND & DRUMS

of the 4th Batt., The Welch Regiment,

by kind permission of Lt.-Col. G. P. Philips, D.L.

Printed by Albert E. Davies. 201. Oxford Street Swansea

(By kind permission of the Gower Agricultural Society).

a man in a green trilby hat spouting on the field, warning that war would be starting any day. Any day was three days later – September 3rd!

We all got dressed up for the show, blancoed our white shoes and wore white socks. The girls had ribbons in their hair and berets, or sometimes panama hats. While the children, and women too I think, dressed in a summery fashion, men wore suits no doubt of quite thick material and including a waistcoat and watch and chain. Some of the older men wore flannel shirts and also bowlers. Most men wore caps or trilbies.

In later years, we children would wander around the whole grounds, and enjoyed bumping in to old friends. Our parents would renew old acquaintances. Familes would have a 'base' where you could sit and leave things. A great number of people sat around the ring where the horse riding events took place. Show jumping in those days was unknown to the ordinary Gower person. My uncle Gower Davies was a postman, and he always took a day's holiday for Show Day – and spent it on the gate. He checked in the vehicles carrying animals. He loved it! As the 'horsey' people came along he greeted them 'Good morning, sir. Good morning, madam!'

An almost equally big attraction were the Sheepdog Trials which I liked to watch. The funniest thing I saw was an exasperated handler, after frustration and failure with his dog, grabbing a last loose sheep and hurling it into the pen!

There wasn't much to spend money on, perhaps a balloon or a flag or one of those streamers with a feather on the end that you could blow out with a buzzing noise. A great treat was ice-cream!

Penrice for me also meant the important people who lived there – and also a person who worked for them, the agent Mr. Prichard. My mother said he was greatly feared by tenants and looked imperious on a white horse. She spoke warmly of Lady Blythswood. I think she had met her in the 1st World War during her training as a nurse. An ancestor of Lady Blythswood was Christopher Rice Mansel Talbot Esq. M.P. Now you won't believe this . . . a large portrait of him hung in our parlour along with one of Queen Victoria! My mother had bought both portraits in a sale, for the frames.

Round the ring, late 1930s.
(By kind permission of Keith Evans).

CHAPTER 3

From 1946-1986

The show was not held during the Second World War; the 31st Show was held on the 29th August 1946.

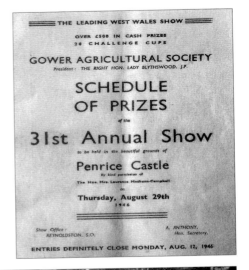

GOWER SHOW, 1946

Gower Show Schedule, 1946.
(By kind permission of Keith Evans).

Norman Richards, Kimley Moor, in his milk cart.
Left is Tom Davies, Scurlage Court.
(By kind permission of John Beynon).

THE BEYNON FAMILY OF GELLIGROES AT THE GOWER SHOW, REMEMBERED BY VALERIE BEYNON

My first memories of the Gower Show were from the late forties – following lines of cattle lorries and horse boxes over Cefn Bryn, arriving early at Penrice to find a good spot for the car near the ringside, meeting so many people – family and friends from all over the peninsula, nervously inspecting the corn and roots section for prize cards and enjoying the warmth of success, visiting the Flower tent (which seemed to take ages!) then back to the Ring for the Grand Parade and the horse jumping. We seemed to be steered clear of the sideshows until the last possible moment. In the early fifties there was no W.I. section so my mother in her enthusiasm for competition encouraged my sister Helen and I to enter the Wild Flower section. The day before was spent travelling the length of Gower – Oxwich for bulrushes, the marsh at Gwernffrwd for marshmallow and viper's bugloss, the old railway line at Penclawdd for wonderful willowherb and purple loosestrife. That was an early lesson in the geography and botany of Gower.

Richard Beynon, Blaencedi.

The Gower Show was an important part of my childhood, as there had been a long family association since the first Show. My grandfather Richard Beynon of Blaencedi, had been involved with the Gower Fat Stock Show held at Reynoldston in December for some years, and he was a member of the organising committee for the first Gower Agricultural Show in 1906. He regularly competed in the corn and roots section, and, always wore the show 'uniform' – a bowler hat. He stewarded in every show from 1906 until his death at 91 in 1957.

Like many farmers' young sons, Aubrey and Benjamin Richard, my father, did not initially share his pioneering enthusiasm and exacting demands in preparing the entries – handpicking the best heads of corn and matching swedes and mangolds for identical size. My father preferred the fun and social side – competing in the horseback games in the ring, on his favourite horse 'Tommy', and then the Dance at the Reynoldston Hall in the evening. Later, when he moved to farm in Gelligroes near Llanmorlais, he became as involved as his father and both he and Aubrey competed (usually against each other) with the same enthusiasm, determination and success as Richard senior. I recall that when the date of the Show was changed from the last to the first Thursday in August, there was some initial concern that, especially for the North Gower farmer, the corn would not be ripe in time for the Show, but with careful selection, good sheaves of wheat, oats and barley duly appeared from the fields. Both sons continued the family tradition of stewarding, and after retirement, judging and in 1958 like his father before him, my father served as a Show Society Officer as Chairman of the Committee.

The show was also an important date in the annual calendar for my mother Elizabeth's family of Bishopston Farm. Her father William Jones, used to exhibit horses and his son, also William, competed (against my father and uncle) in corn and roots. As soon as the Women's Institute cookery section started in the late 1920s, my mother and her sister Gladys became very keen competitors. That gave them such pleasure and confidence that it lead to their establishment of Bishopston W.I. in 1932 and both achieved great success in the W.I. movement.

Marjorie Williams, Peggy Shepherd and Mrs. Fanny Williams,
Woodlands, Llanrhidian, at the Gower Show in 1947.
(By kind permission of Mrs. T. Pritchard).

'Notabilities at the Gower Show',
Evening Post, Friday, 5th September 1947.
Standing from left – Rev. W. Jones, Mr. G. H. Rowlands, Mr. A. Anthony
(Secretary), the Hon. Laurence Methuen-Campbell, Sir Robert Webber,
Sir William Jenkins, Mr. George Jenkins, Major D. C. Smartt,
Col. F. S. Morgan and Mr. G. Beynon.
In front – Jean, Wendy and David Methuen-Campbell.

GOWER SHOW, 1947
From left – Gordon Deacon, Arwyn Lewis, Gwynder Lewis.
On car – Susan Cohen, Tim Lewis, Mike Piercey, Gloria Jenkins,
Rowland Jenkins, Jane Piercey.
(By kind permission of Mrs. Gloria MacLeod).

G. I. Thomas, haulier of Llanrhidian,
at the Gower Show, 1947.
(By kind permission of Mrs. Ivy Griffiths).

GOWER SHOW, 1948
'Tysill Dreadnaught', owned by Mr. Dick Clement, Freedown Farm.
From left – Betty, Dick and Janie Clement.
(By kind permission of Mrs. Janie Clement).

THE GOWER SHOW
REMEMBERED BY JANIE HUTIN (NÉE CLEMENT)
OF FREEDOWN FARM, LLANRHIDIAN

On Gower Show day, most Gower people would make time to go to it. It was a holiday in a way, and only the jobs that had to be carried out on the farm were done. As children, my sister Betty and myself would walk, with our parents Dick and Bessie Clement from Freedown Farm, over Cefn Bryn to the Show in Penrice. It was a very exciting place to be! The grounds were very busy, and there were lots of places to explore – with the animals and produce, and wonderful things to see in the Flower and W.I. tents. There was the Sheepdog Trials, Show Jumping, all the Trade Stands with the new machinery, and not forgetting the shows (or fairground rides) at the entrance to the field. They must have been a trial to all parents! It was a wonderful time, (weather permitting) but the biggest treat of all was to sit under the trees and have a packet of crisps and a bottle of pop to drink. Today's children would not be very impressed with that sort of treat!

My father was always one of the Stewards with the sheep, but not the year we took the bull to the show. During the Second World War there was no show. It returned in 1946. It must have been a difficult time for everyone in 1948 as entries were low, so the Secretary, Mr. Arthur Anthony, asked my father if he could bring an animal to the show to help make up the numbers in the different classes. We had just bought a new bull. We had always kept a bull for our own cows and those of our neighbours. We decided to take him to the show. Betty and I had to go with my father, so George Thomas and his lorry was hired. It was a very wet morning so Macs and Wellingtons were the order of the day. Our bull, Tysill Dreadnaught, a shorthorn came fourth – there were only four in the class! We didn't get a prize, but we had plenty of excitement. The bull got free, but luckily for us Richard James, Llandewi had stock close by, and he managed to catch him for us, so then he was tied up a bit sounder. We couldn't blame him for wanting to run away – it was raining heavily all the time, we had to empty our Wellingtons as they had filled with water. We were very wet and miserable, we couldn't leave the bull alone, so had to stay close to him until all the animals were allowed to be taken home. We didn't see anything of the show that day, but we were given the photograph because the photographer thought it was the best one he had taken at the show.

In later years, my husband Selwyn and I went to the show with our children. Once or twice I was a steward in the W.I. tent. It is a good thing to have it back in Penrice, as when it was at the Aerodrome it didn't feel like the Gower Show.

'A wet day for the show. How about a drink?' was the caption on this photograph, which appeared in the *Herald of Wales* on the 4th September 1948.

PENRICE ESTATE OFFICE
REMEMBERED BY BETTY DOHERTY

I started work in the Estate office in 1945, and went on to work there for forty-two years – the only job I ever had!

Mr. Anthony the agent did all the accounts in his office, and I worked in the outer office. He lived at Hayes Cottage in Reynoldston. He had been a founder member of the Gower Show and its secretary for forty-five years.

Once we started on the preparations for the Gower Show it was all go! The first thing to be done was to get the Schedule of all the classes prepared for printing, and updating such things as Awards etc., from the previous year. The Sponsors had to be contacted and asked if they wanted to be included in the new Schedules and Catalogues. When all the details were completed, they were taken to the printers. On receipt of the Schedules they were posted to each competitor.

GOWER SHOW, 1949

From right – Margaret M. Jones, Betty Doherty and George Long, *Evening Post*.
(By kind permission of Mrs. Doherty, formerly of Horton).

As the entries for the Classes came in, they were entered into a ledger, with a page for each class. There was a date limit for entries, except for the Sheepdog Trials and Horse Jumping. These were accepted on the Show Day. All this information was again taken to the printers with an order for the estimated amount required.

Judges and visiting personalities were contacted and if they required accommodation for the night of the Show, this had to be arranged for them. Caterers had to be organised, also the Police and First Aid personnel. New badges were ordered for everyone – from the President to stewards for the current year – together with rosettes, prize cards, luncheon tickets, vouchers, car park tickets, entry tickets, vehicle passes and members' tickets.

We had to contact the men who erected all the various rings, and also organise toilet facilities in the ruins of the old Penrice Castle, which are at the far end of Penrice Park. Marquees, tents and structures had to be hired for various organisations.

We also had to contact all trophy and cup winners to remind them to return them. Most of them did – but we had to chase up a few!

When all these things were done, we hoped for a fine day. A dance was always held in Reynoldston Hall in the evening of the Show day.

I must say, however, that whilst all the preparations were going on, our first priority was the day-to-day business of the Penrice Estate.

71

Herald of Wales, 3rd September 1949.
Miss Nott, Pennard Riding School, with Michael Williams and Roger Hayes.

OFFICIALS AND GUESTS AT THE GOWER SHOW 1950s.
Front row from left – Mr. G. Lewis; Mrs. D. R. Grenfell; Mr. D. R. Grenfell, M.P.;
Lady Blythswood; the Mayor and Mayoress of Swansea, Councillor and
Mrs. D. J. Fisher, and Lady Jenkins. Second row – Ernest Richards;
Capt. H. Leighton Davies; Mr. D. L. Mort, M.P. and Mrs. Mort;
Alderman Percy Morris, M.P; Mrs. G. Lewis; Sir William Jenkins;
Mrs. R. S. Palmer; David Methuen-Campbell, and Gwilym Pugh.
Amongst those in the back row are – George Davies; Col. F. S. Morgan;
Mr. R. S. Palmer; George Jenkins; Mr. and Mrs. C. Methuen-Campbell,
and members of Mr. Methuen-Campbell's family.
(By kind permission of Donald Lewis).

David John Jones, chauffeur to Sir William and Lady Jenkins.
(By kind permission of Gareth Jones).

A TRIP TO THE GOWER SHOW
REMEMBERED BY GARETH JONES

My father, David John Jones, was chauffeur to Sir William and Lady Jenkins (seen in the preceding photograph) in the late 1950s and early 1960s. I recall accompanying my father when he took Sir William and Lady Jenkins to the Gower Show. Sir William was a significant figure in Swansea, and served as its Mayor in 1947.

The Humber Super Snipe had a coat of arms on the door, and I remember that policemen and RAC/AA officers would salute as the car went by.

When we arrived at the Showground, my father would drive to the main ring, and the car would be parked, bonnet facing inwards, so that Sir William and Lady Jenkins could watch the proceedings for a while. They would later meet the other dignitaries and attend the official luncheon.

I remember feeling very privileged to travel in such style, and wear a member's badge. I was always fascinated by the show jumping, and would head for the ring to watch the competitors there.

GOWER SHOW, 1950
From left – Lily Bennett, Frances Evans, Esther Bowen, Lovain Bennett
and Ivy Evans.
(By kind permission of Glyn Rogers).

GOWER SHOW, 1950s
Included here are Ivor Davies, M.P.; Mr. and Mrs. C. Methuen-Campbell;
Col. Morgan; Mr. and Mrs. Glyn Hughes, Landimore, and far right
Patrick McNair Wilson, M.P.
(By kind permission of Mrs. Hazel Williams).

The committee minute book of 1951 records a proposition that the sheep-dog trials should be run on the National style instead of the South Wales style, which would mean that the dogs would have to fetch the sheep and drive them away. It was felt that this should encourage sheepdog owners from outside the immediate area to compete.

It was decided that the trials should follow the usual South Wales style in the morning and the National style in the afternoon.

SHEEPDOG TRIALS
BY EMRYS EVANS, SCURLAGE CASTLE

I was senior steward on the sheep for many years. The trials were always done in the South Wales style. Three sheep were used for the competition. The dog had to pick up the sheep, and then drive them through different shaped gates.

It was then decided to change the event to the South Wales style in the morning and National style in the afternoon.

For National style, five sheep were used. The dog had to drive them around three different gates, bring them back for shedding and shed the one wearing the black collar. They were then penned.

Competitors would travel quite a distance to compete, but would often go to a few shows the same day. One year they were still competing in Penrice at 9.30 in the evening!

I have seen some competitors run both styles. Dai Daniels from the Swansea Valleys ran both and won the National Championship.

The other sheep stewards with me were Glanville Davies, John Pritchard and Tom Evans.

GOWER SHOW, 1950s

Mrs. Oona Methuen-Campbell presenting a cup for the best roots to Norman Richards, Kimley Moor.

(By kind permission of John Beynon).

GOWER SHOW, 1951
(By kind permission of Robert Davies, Knelston).

'George the Giant' was on display in a tent at the 1951 Show, and a charge
was made for admission. 'George', an eight-year-old South Devon bullock,
weighed 35 cwts. and measured 17 hands.
(By kind permission of Mrs. Hazel Williams).

Gower Show morning at Pitt Farm, Penrice,
early 1950s. Arthur Evans with his
sheaves of corn.
(By kind permission of Mrs. Olwen Evans).

Rachel, Rosalind and Sarah Evans, Pitt Farm, with their flowers.
(By kind permission of Mrs. Olwen Evans).

GOWER SHOW, 1951

Robert Davies, Margaret Jones, Ron Maddoc and Sylvia Jones.
(By kind permission of Mrs. Margaret Davies).

Dai Jones, Cillibion (centre, in white coat), with his prize-winning cow.
(By kind permission of Mrs. Sylvia Long).

GOWER SHOW, EARLY 1950s

From left – Donald Button, Rhossili, Emrys Jones, Lunnon, Glyn Rogers, Kennexstone, William Jones, Lunnon, Bill James, Wick (Judge), John Williams, Big House Farm, Lunnon (behind judge), unknown, Arthur Evans, Pitt Farm, and David Edwards, Stonemill, Parkmill.

(By kind permission of V. Jones, Lunnon).

EMRYS JONES, LUNNON

I remember one show in which I had entered a sheaf of white oats. The judge, who had spent some time making his mind up, came to me carrying two sheaves and said, 'It's my belief that these sheaves are from the same field!'

I was of the same belief – as we had found tracks through our field! However, the judge had to make a decision, though the two sheaves were identical. I came second!

DENNIS COOKE, FORMERLY OF THE BAYS FARM, OVERTON, REMEMBERS THE GOWER SHOW OF THE 1950s

During the greater part of this decade, I was working with my grand-mother Mrs. Lydia Stevens and her son (my uncle) Ernest Stevens at The Bays Farm, Overton. My uncle had been prominent in Gower Show circles for many years and in particular with the showing of Ryeland sheep, and also of roots in the Corn and Roots section.

Two neighbouring farmers were also keen show enthusiasts and there was intense but good-hearted rivalry between us. These neighbours were J. M. Jones, Newhouse Farm, and Len Jeffreys, Bay View Farm. J. M. Jones showed Suffolk sheep and Len Jeffreys showed the same breed, but I think he may have shown Clun Forest in earlier years.

Whilst each would enter in their respective breed classes, the rivalry would come to a head when it came to competing for the perpetual trophies (held for one year only and then returned), for the Best Ram in Show and Best Ram Lamb in Show, etc.

Other Gower competitors in the 'Down' breeds were Glyn M. James & Sons, Llandewi Castle, showing Suffolks, as did E. R. Jones & Sons, of East Pilton. A. B. Turnbull, Home Farm, showed Clun Forest. Friendly rivalry in the 'Hill' breeds came from outside Gower. Well known were two from Velindre – Evans, Cwrt Mawr, and Pethrick, Ffynnon Fedw, showing Welsh Mountain. From farther afield came Morgan, Eglwys-wrw, showing Kerry Hill.

In the class entitled 'Any other breed', those stalwarts, Jasper & Bertram Watters, Oxwich Castle, would almost be guaranteed to win by entering breeds from other parts of the U.K. that we had hardly heard of, such as Teeswater and Derbyshire Gritstone.

Ernest Stevens checking his Ryeland flock for a potential winner.
(By kind permission of Dennis Cooke).

Preparation of sheep for showing started well in advance of the show season. Our Ryelands lambed mainly in February/early March, and my uncle would have his eye on one or two ram lambs from about six weeks of age – particularly if their dams had been successful in previous years. Getting sheep used to being handled and haltered was part of the preparation. Shearing was done early in the year so that by the time of the show season, neatly trimmed animals would materialise. Getting matched pairs of ewes and ewe lambs took considerable skill, and getting three was even more difficult.

In the week immediately prior to the Show, there would be much time spent on final trimming, combing and patting plus letting them run out without getting wet!

The showing of 'root crops' refers to crops grown for fodder – principally mangolds (or 'mangels'), swedes and turnips. Mangolds were the largest of the three crops. Swedes and turnips grown for fodder were larger than those we see today used for culinary purposes.

Mangolds have disappeared from the scene today because they were exceptionally labour intensive to grow and harvest. Mangolds were the most attractive of the group, being mostly large globe shaped with a relatively clean crown and small neck of leaves. There were three main types – lemon globe, orange globe and long red, all of them being whitish – yellowish fleshed. My uncle, Ernest Stevens favoured the lemon globe for showing. Our neighbours favoured the orange globe.

To show the roots required matching six of the same. 2, 3, or 4 were difficult enough, but 6 – a headache! One of the rules of entry was that your exhibit came from land in your control on which you grew at least ¼ acre of each type.

My uncle would go to outrageous lengths to get 6 matching mangolds. I well remember going out with him at dusk (when he thought the neighbours would not be watching) – putting down a pinch of sulphate of ammonia around the mangolds he had earlier marked with sticks, as being likely to make show specimens. He would also carefully clean the necks of any surplus rough growth.

Swedes were easier to match – or seemed to be! He always grew the variety 'Lord Warden'. Likewise, turnips were relatively easy to match. Sometimes, the same sets of 6 could be exhibited at other shows on the circuit – provided the judge had not cut one open to see if it was hollow inside!

Moving the date of the Gower Show from the first Thursday in September to early in August did not help the root section because it reduced the period of maturity.

Ernest Stevens with his prize-winning mangolds.
(By kind permission of Dennis Cooke).

Gordon Griffiths showing the pony of J. Gilbert at the Gower Show, 1951.
(By kind permission of Gordon Griffiths).

K. Crumpton, Betty Doherty and Les March
at the 1951 Gower Show.
(By kind permission of Mrs. Betty Doherty).

GOWER SHOW, 1952
Michael Phillips, Julian Griffiths, Doreen, Glenys
and Jacqueline Jeffreys, in pushchair is Jeff Griffiths, Llanrhidian.
(By kind permission of Mrs. Ivy Griffiths).

GUESTS AT THE LUNCHEON OF THE 1955 GOWER SHOW
Included in front row – Councillor I. A. Gronow, Chairman of Gower RDC
and Mrs. Gronow; the Mayor and Mayoress of Swansea, Alderman and
Mrs. F. C. Jones; Mr. and Mrs. B. James, and Mrs. Hewlett.
Back row – Mr. Sidney Heath, Mr. C. Methuen-Campbell,
Supt. J. Hewlett, and Mrs. Heath.
(By kind permission of the Gower Agricultural Society).

Michael Beynon,
Llanrhidian,
at the 1955 Gower Show.
*(By kind permission of
Mrs. Edna Beynon).*

Bryn Williams, Reynoldston.
(By kind permission of Mrs. Elizabeth Dyson).

B.C. OR 'BRYN THE BEES'
REMEMBERED BY HIS DAUGHTER, LIZ DYSON

August was always a special time in our household as the day of the Gower Show drew closer. This day was talked about for weeks before – and even the winter months were spent working towards Show Day.

My parents kept bees, so I lived in a bee-friendly environment – bee-hives in the garden and throughout Gower, and boxes piled high in the kitchen holding honey that would soon be extracted and poured into jars. There was also wax for moulds, candles and beeswax polish, and mead – a heady combination of honey and fermented water, flavoured with the pollen from the field, hedgerow and meadow.

From the age of 13, my father became fascinated with the honeybee, and his enthusiasm continued to the end of his days, ably supported by my mother, who during the war years when he was on active service, looked after the bees until his return.

In my memory, the day of the Gower Show was always sunny. It was a day that brought friends and family together, and I remember so well the many people who sat in the sunshine sharing picnic food and dressed in their best clothes. This was an occasion to live up to!

85

The honey tent was full of exhibits, such as an observation hive with the marked queen. My father would delight in sharing his knowledge and sparking interest wherever possible.

I remember with affection this special day of the year, and as it drew to a close, my parents would already be making plans for the next year's show.

THE W.I. SECTION OF THE GOWER SHOW FROM 1957 BY VALERIE BEYNON, REYNOLDSTON

When the Gower Show restarted in 1946, there was great disappointment that there would be no cookery classes because of rationing. In 1957 when my mother – Elizabeth Beynon, Gelligroes – was a member of the Glamorgan County W.I. Executive and first organiser of the Produce Guild, she was invited by Ernest Richards to restart the W.I. section, funded by the Show Society but conforming to W.I. standards. A new local committee was formed which included Nelly Jefford, Reynoldston (Chairman), Violet Morgan, Llanrhidian, Netta Chalk, Rhossili, Glenis Lucas, Llanrhidian, and Elizabeth Beynon, Llanmorlais. My mother later served as Chairman for thirty years and finally retired in 1996 (aged 85!) when the cookery section became open to any competitor. In 2003 just before she died, she was delighted to know that the W.I. cooperative section was going to be reintroduced. On her retirement she was presented with a hand painted plate from the Society and the Committee at that time included Joyce Brown, who was a tireless secretary, Kathleen Pritchard, Vice-Chairman, with Marjorie Bardell, Kay Beynon, Lily Davies, Daphne Furneaux, Celia Grove, Angela Howells, Anona Morris, Brenda Talbot, Gwenda Taylor and Brenda Thomas.

My mother loved the organisation of the W.I. tent. A Committee meeting was held in January each year to decide the schedule contents and the topical theme for the co-operative. From then until August every jar of preserve was carefully produced with immaculate lines of fruit in case it 'might do for the Show'. The best jams and marmalade were hidden away and there would be much dismay if used by accident. In July there would be meetings to allocate tasks and test the results of those W.I. members who had agreed (or been invited!) to contribute to the co-operative. Constructing the set required a high level of DIY skills since marks were allocated for staging and presentation and this often caused more worry than the food preparation. In the last few days there would be lots of trial cakes and tarts to be tasted. The committee would

Mrs. Elizabeth Beynon.
(By kind permission of Valerie Beynon).

meet the evening before (as the section grew in later years with so many entries this would take all day) to prepare the tables and allocate spaces. Sometimes there were insufficient tables or they were not up to the standard and there would be negotiations with Mr. Lesley Marsh of the Show Office or the Show Director. When the Show moved to the airport site, the W.I. tent was much larger and the committee was very pleased to have more space. Returning home late after this preparation of the tent, there would be last minute baking, especially of Welsh cakes – and polishing of jars.

The Show day meant an early arrival at the grounds. As the W.I. members set out their entries with a quick glance at their rivals', there was a buzz and not a little nervousness. The tent was then cleared – not easily – for what seemed like hours of judging. Usually around 2 p.m. a queue would develop outside and eventually the tent would be open and the results known. There would be much excited laughter for the winners and particularly from the W.I. members who had won the co-operative where the rivalry was keenest. There were regularly 14 or 15 W.I.'s competing and in the early days Newton always seemed to win, but by careful study of its success, others 'caught on' and soon Bishopston, Llanmorlais, Rhossili, Llandewi and all the others triumphed in turn to hold the Gladys Griffiths Memorial Cup. There were also more than 500 individual entries and the Gelligroes Cup was awarded to the Institute whose members gained the highest total of points.

The first W.I. section in the 1920s had started with handicraft and needlework competitions, and, guided by Miss Doris Richards of Penmaen, this was also restarted in 1957 and painting and photography were added. The combined attraction of the cookery and craft made the tent extremely popular and crowded. Movement was slow because the work had to be admired, the results examined – who did well and reading the judges' comments – and conversations had to be continued from the previous year! The atmosphere summed up what the Gower Show was about. My mother only left the tent for luncheon.

In 1990, she was honoured to be elected the first lady Vice-President of the Gower Agricultural Society for her role in the success of the W.I. section. She loved the W.I. part of the Show for its achievement in raising standards and for the confidence and encouragement it gave W.I. members but above all for helping to maintain a community spirit in the villages and throughout Gower.

Pat Smythe at the 1958 Gower Show.
(By kind permission of Mrs. Gwyneth Thomas).

Pat Smythe had discharged herself from hospital after a painful fall, in order to compete in the 1958 Gower Show.

GOWER SHOW 1958
From left – Judy Davies, Wendy Darly, Elizabeth Tucker and Pauline Tucker.
(By kind permission of Mrs. Gwyneth Thomas).

Evelyn and Byron Tucker with their son Martin
at the 1958 Gower Show.
(By kind permission of George Tucker, Llanrhidian).

Glyn Hughes, Landimore, with his 1959 Gower Show prize-winning pony.
(By kind permission of Mrs. Hazel Williams).

SHEEPDOG TRIALS
Standing left – Ernie Beynon and Colin Gordon. Seated – E. J. Evans (Judge),
Benny Jones, Llethryd. Standing right – Les Jones, Pontardulais,
Lyn Lewis, Ystradgynlais, E. L. Davies, Ystradgynlais.
(By kind permission of Ernie Beynon, Rhossili).

THE GOWER SHOW, 1959
REMEMBERED BY ERNIE BEYNON, RHOSSILI

I remember when we went to the Gower Show in our old blue van in 1959. We took three fatstock Welsh Mountain ewe lambs in the back with my dog Nell, and my daughter's pushchair. We were all squashed up in the front! I found the sheep pens and then parked the van in the shade under the trees and we went to watch the sheepdog trials. Benny Jones, then of Wernffrwd came up to me to ask if I had my dog in the van. He explained that although there were a lot of entries in the sheep-dog competition, there were three shows on the same day – in Abergavenny, Gower and Pembroke – and many of the competitors would go to all the shows, so would not arrive in Gower until it was time for them to participate. There was very little in the meantime for the crowds to watch. I said I would give her a run, but I didn't hold out much hope, as although she was good at bringing the sheep down off Rhossili Hill, she had never even seen a Maltese Cross!

She went off and worked well, and at the end of the competition we came second! The dog that beat her had cost more than my van, so I was really proud of her.

When I went to pick up the ewes, I found that they had won first prize. It was quite a successful show!

I entered the sheepdog trials in the following year with much more confidence – and the sheep ended up on the toilet roof in the Old Ruins!

William Roderick, Bank Farm, Scurlage,
with his prize-winning Hereford.
(By kind permission of Mrs. V. Roderick).

91

Herefords from the Brangwyn Herd, Bank Farm, Scurlage. Late 1950s.
(By kind permission of Mrs. V. Roderick).

John Roderick, Bank Farm, Scurlage.
(By kind permission of Mrs. V. Roderick).

GOWER SHOW, 1961

The prize-winners' cups, ready for presentation. First left is Gwilym Pugh,
second left Marsden Jones, 4th left George Richards.
(By kind permission of John Morgan, Reynoldston).

Morgan Jones, at the 1961 Gower Show.
(By kind permission of John Morgan, Reynoldston).

Whitbread brewery horses at the 1961 Gower Show.
(By kind permission of John Morgan, Reynoldston).

Cattle in the 1961 show ring.
(By kind permission of John Morgan, Reynoldston).

Show jumping competition 1961.
(By kind permission of John Morgan, Reynoldston).

1963 Gower Show prize-winner – Jack Leeke of Llanrhidian.
(By kind permission of Mrs. Hazel Williams).

Stephen Tucker of Rock House, Llanrhidian, with the bull 'Brocket Ringer' in 1964. The bull belonged to his grandfather Haydn Parry of Monksland Farm, and was from the herd of Lord Brockett. Haydn Parry's herd was known as Glengower Herefords. Also present – Tina Elliot, Dunraven, and Frances Edwards, Llanmadoc.
(By kind permission of Mrs. Jean Tucker, Llanrhidian).

GOWER SHOW, 1964
From left – 'Faeni Stud' – Mathias. 'Treharne Tomboy' – Geoff Williams. 'Coed Coch Penrhyn' – Aubrey Oliver. Judge: Mrs. Yeoman.
(By kind permission Aubrey Oliver).

Margaret Oliver with 'Coed Coch Persawr'
at the 1964 Gower Show.
(By kind permission of Aubrey Oliver).

A. B. TURNBULL
REMEMBERED BY AUBREY OLIVER

Alan Turnbull was a Yorkshireman born and bred. During World War II he had worked for the Ministry of Agriculture. He then came to Gower to farm, and was a tenant of the Home Farm on the Penrice Estate. In my opinion, he was the kingpin of Gower farming – a considerate employer who ran his farm like a mini-factory. He was a disappointed man if he didn't get two crops from each of his fields! He later farmed Oxwich Castle Farm as well, and employed a staff of 18 men – besides the casual labourers.

Mr. A. B. Turnbull.
(By kind permission of the Gower Agricultural Society).

He was the Director of the Gower Show from 1951 until the 1980s and organised it with great precision. He used his labour force – without charge – to prepare the show ground the week before the Show, and during the day of the Show worked tirelessly to ensure that everything ran smoothly. He had amazing energy and was always on the go!

As a man, he was held in high regard in Gower and his opinion was always well respected.

Gillian Grove with one of
Ernest Stevens' Ryelands at the
1964 Gower Show.
(By kind permission of Mrs. Grove).

Carey Jenkins (later Knox), aged 10,
winner of the 1965 Gower Show's
children's riding pony section.
(By kind permission of Mrs. C. Knox).

GOWER SHOW, 1960s
John Hutin with his daughter Janet riding Dick Beynon's pony 'Berwick Cocoa'.
(By kind permission of Mrs. J. Eynon-Davies).

GOWER SHOW OFFICIALS, 1966
Standing, from left – Capt. Leighton Davies, Supt. and Mrs. Hewlett,
Mrs. Rees Jones, Mr. Bernard Hastie, Dr. Rees Jones,
and Mr. David Methuen-Campbell.
Seated, from left – Mr. and Mrs. John Pritchard, Mr. and Mrs. Jack Richards,
Mr. and Mrs. C. Methuen-Campbell, Mrs. Ivor Davies and Mr. Ivor Davies, M.P.
(By kind permission of the Gower Agricultural Society).

Left – Graham Davies with a Hereford bull from Long Oaks Farm,
and Meredith Kneath showing Sam Jeffreys' Hereford bull.
(By kind permission of Gordon Griffiths).

GOWER SHOW, 1966
'Gredlington Bleworg' with Aubrey Oliver.
Amongst the onlookers are Mr. Pugh,
Vet. Surgeon, and Ted Davies, Pontlasse.
(By kind permission of Aubrey Oliver).

Catherine Williams,
aged 3, at the 1968 Gower
Show, holding the
photographer's monkey.
*(By kind permission of
Mrs. C. Heather).*

Champion Hereford Bull from Betlands Farm held by Roger Davies,
with David and Ellis Davies.
(By kind permission of A. Ellis Davies).

THOUSANDS FLOCK TO RECORD-BREAKING GOWER SHOW . . .

BUMPER to bumper, thousands flocked to this year's record-breaking annual Gower Show at Penrice on Thursday. From the start it looked like a huge success as queues of cars lined all the approach roads to the showground.

Traffic stretched for miles throughout the day and for the first time cars had to be turned away from the main show car park.

By early afternoon the vast grounds were packed with visitors enjoying the brilliant sunshine and the show's events and exhibitions. The main crowd-pullers were the sheepdog trials, dog show and horse jumping—in which Alan Oliver, Oriel Ferguson and Fred Broome took part.

£1,750 in prizes

With prizes totalling £1,750 and numerous cups and rosettes to be won, competition in all events was high.

The show's director, Mr. A. B. Turnbull, said: "We are all very pleased at the way it has turned out and there is no doubt that it has been a record-breaker.

"It has been a record financially as well as attendance-wise, but it is difficult to say how much the takings are up because of this year's increased charges.

For the first time ever we have had to turn cars away at the main gate, but we were able to provide alternative car parking for them.

"The standard of this year's show was very high and the horse competitions were excellent. Judging by the car number plates the visitors must have come from far afield.

"The only problems we had was with the number of cars."

Alan Oliver, winner of the Everest double glazing stakes, is presented with a horse rug by Mr. F. Bassett-Jones, regional sales manager of Everest Double Glazing Home Insulation Ltd.

Herald of Wales, August 14th 1971.
Thousands flock to record-breaking Gower Show.

Bumper to bumper!

Steven, Ann and Caroline Jones around the main ring in 1973.
(By kind permission of Roger Jones, formerly of Cillibion).

THE GOWER SHOW
REMEMBERED BY ROGER JONES, CILLIBION

The Gower Show resumed in 1946 after the war, and my parents, George and Marjorie Jones of Cillibion, went every year from then onwards. We always purchased our tickets from Hazel Williams, Oldwalls, who in the annual returns would be shown as one of the most successful collectors in Gower.

In the 1940s, just a track led down through the estate, and it was great entertainment after heavy rain to watch the mud-bound cars being towed out by tractors. The funfair was down by the Castle, and we were allowed to roam around the Castle walls.

By the time of the 1960s, we would always have to arrive early – usually about 8 a.m. – so that we could park in 'our place' on the edge of the Show ring. In those days cars were allowed around the ring, and everyone had their favourite spot. We would set up folding chairs, and always had the same families alongside us. We took two hampers –one for lunch and one for tea. As the years went by, we had to leave home earlier and earlier to get to 'our spot.' One year we left at 6 a.m.

My wife and I continued to go the Show with our family, until it moved to the airport. I am delighted that it is now back in Penrice, and we were so pleased to celebrate the Show's centenary in its rightful home.

GOWER SHOW, 1975

Chris Stokes, Overton, with 10-week-old 'Telstar'.
(By kind permission of Mrs. C. Evans).

Milwyn Layton and John Furneaux, Gower Show, 1975.
(By kind permission of Milwyn Layton).

Gower Show, 1975. Elwyn Rees with 'Gower Princess'.
(By kind permission of Miss Gladys Hughes).

'Gower Glory' led by Elwyn Rees.
(By kind permission of Miss Gladys Hughes).

Miss Gladys Hughes pictured with 'Gower Warrior'.
(By kind permission of Miss Gladys Hughes).

Andrew Evans showing 'Gower Warrior'.
(By kind permission of Miss Gladys Hughes).

Newton W.I. members arriving at the
W.I. tent, Gower Show 1978.
From left – Peggy Hughes, Joyce Brown
and Jean Williams.
(By kind permission of Newton W.I.).

Ian Balsdon, announcer in the
Gower Show in the 1970s and
early 1980s. He was also
chief announcer in the
Royal Welsh Show.
(By kind permission of Gill Balsdon).

GOWER GOATS BY MARY GWYNNE, FORMERLY OF MALTHOUSE FARM, PENGWERN

Nancy Brook (Brookie) from New Parc, Llanrhidian, and Mary Gwynne from Malthouse Farm, Pengwern, enjoyed keeping goats and sharing important information about them and were keen to let people know how wonderful goats were to keep.

Goats are the most productive animals for their size, and their goats at this time were giving an average of a gallon a day of top quality milk. The milk is known to help in the treatment of many skin conditions in humans and is excellent for babies and children who are allergic to cows milk. Both also enjoyed making their own cheese for their family and friends. Mary and her husband Cyril kept their billy kids for meat. They also cured the skins for rugs.

Mrs. N. Brook (Brookie) in the ring (centre) with judges.
(By kind permission of Mrs. N. Brook).

The Gower Show had never had a goat section, so Brookie and Mary set out to see if they could establish one. They asked the Gower show committee, who were a little apprehensive to start with and did not see the need for the expense of a marquee for the goats, believing that they could be penned outside. This is what Brookie and Mary wanted to change. They wanted the Gower Show to be one of the top goat shows in Britain by providing a milk recording competition as well as judging the look of the animal. Competitors would sleep overnight with their goats, as there would be a judge there in the evening before the show to check the 'stripping out' of udders at milking time. The next day, all milk would not only be weighed for amount but also tested for butterfat content. The quality is as important as the quantity. Goats with good butterfat content and good yields can display star and dagger marks on their pedigree certificates.

The show committee eventually agreed, so Brookie and Mary set up a goat committee. Brookie had recently set up a Glamorganshire goat society, that had active members in Gower, and they became the stalwarts of the Gower Show goat section. Anita and John Grove from the Common, Llanrhidian, were already keeping top class goats, so their help was invaluable, Annie Morris from Three Crosses was a great support and Adrian Hughes from Reynoldston was a very enthusiastic young helper. Of course, behind every good wife there is a worn out husband. Brookie and Mary's husbands – Jim and Cyril – drove, fetched, carried, and painted hurdles.

Cyril and Mary Gwynne, with 'New Parc Snowdrop'.
(By kind permission of Mrs. M. Gwynne).

The first show was a great success with competitors coming from far and wide. Over the years it went from strength to strength, being recognised by the British Goat Society as one of the best goat shows in Britain, with as many as 170 entries for 24 classes and goats became the largest section of the Gower Show.

The team did everything. They dealt with entries, set up the equipment for milk recording, borrowed and painted pens, made notice boards, designed and printed catalogues, organised sponsors and cups.

Information was collected and provided on all aspects of goat keeping from practical tips to homeopathy and natural rearing. One of the competitors ran a goat farm and set up a stall selling milk and cheese. There were also stalls selling food and equipment for goat keeping.

Annie Morris' organising skills came in handy, she set up a kitchen tent and fed all the competitors, judges and stewards with an evening meal, a full cooked breakfast, lunch and tea and coffee.

She even managed to show a goat or two!

Mrs. Annie Morris in the goat tent, Gower Show 1979.
(By kind permission of Mrs. M. Gwynne).

1982 Gower Show. Emma Bladen with 'Treasure'.
(By kind permission of Mrs. Edna Beynon).

1983 Gower Show. Open Jumping Competition.
1st Prize winner – Martin Williams riding 'St. Peter'.
(By kind permission of Mrs. P. Williams).

Carey Knox, with her son Justin riding 'Fieldcote Pillbox',
winner of the 1984 Supreme Champion of the Show.
(By kind permission of Mrs. C. Knox).

GOWER SHOW, 1985

Ian Smith, with Gladys Tucker, Old Henllys, and their Suffolk ram.
In the background are Deane Gordon, Tyle House, and boxer Colin Jones.
(By kind permission of Miss Gladys Tucker).

Janet Smith with her Texel ram.
(By kind permission of Miss Gladys Tucker).

A picnic at Penrice for, from left – Val Williams, Enid Morgan, Averil Phillips,
Sue Phillips and Emrys Jones of Lunnon Farm.
(By kind permission of Emrys Jones).

In 1987 the Show moved from Penrice to Fairwood Airport.

CHAPTER 4

The Gower Show at Fairwood, 1987-2001

Aerial view of the show.
(By kind permission of Peter Muxworthy).

The band of the Royal British Legion.

GOWER AGRICULTURAL SOCIETY COMMITTEE, 1988

Back row, from left – John Davies, Phillip John, Robert James, Gordon Mitchell, John Beynon, Dick Beynon, Ernest Smith, Kathy Frame, Alison Grove, Hazel Williams, Terry Thomas, and Col. C. Rosser John.

Middle row, from left – Mr. Phillips, Gordon Griffiths, Mr. Hughes, Ernest Jones, John Tucker, Billy Gambold, Benny James.

Front row, from left – Peter Muxworthy, Paul Tucker, John Furneaux, Ernest Richards, John Pritchard, Alan Turnbull, Gill Balsdon.

(By kind permission of the Gower Agricultural Society).

(By kind permission of Mrs. K. Frame).

GOWER SHOW COMMITTEE, 1990s
Back row from left – Ernest Jones, David Methuen-Campbell, John Furneaux,
W. Gambold and Peter Muxworthy.
Front row – Mrs. D. Methuen-Campbell, Morgan Jones, Ernest Richards,
Mrs. Gill Balsdon, Benny James, and John Tucker, Horton.
(By kind permission of the Gower Agricultural Society).

CATTLE

Rosie Grace Tucker, The Beeches, Horton.

Wendy Morgan being presented with a prize-winner's cup
by Mrs. Gwyneth Jones, Lunnon.

Matthew Bevan, aged 6, with 'Isma'
the beef heifer from Berry, Gower,
who took first prize in the
under 24 months class
at the 1995 Gower Show.

Linda Grove, Lady Ambassador to
the Royal Welsh Agricultural Society,
presents the Lady Blythswood Cup
to Richard Tucker, Horton.

Paul Jones, Wernffrwd.

POULTRY

Ronald Tucker of Penclawdd with his white Leghorn
hen that was judged Best Bird in the
1994 Gower Show, by poultry judge Desmond Little.

POULTRY KEEPING
REMEMBERED BY RONALD TUCKER, PENCLAWDD

It was my uncle Robert Guy who first got me interested in poultry.
He used to show Leghorns. I went to the National Show in Olympia,
London with Robert John Davies and his son, Councillor Phillip Davies.
I saw a Leghorn hen there that was Champion in its class. It belonged to
a Scotsman named William Binney. At the time, there had been an outbreak of fowl pest, and although competitors were allowed to bring
their birds into England, when the show was over they couldn't return
to Scotland. I bought the bird, and brought it back to Penclawdd. It won
many local shows, and I began to breed from it.

My uncle William Tucker had been showing birds for years, but had
lost interest, but when I began to breed them, he used to have the pullets.
He would win with his pullets and I would win with the cockerels. We
both won classes at the National Show in Olympia with our birds.

I would prepare the birds for the show by bathing them in Lux soap,
and would add a little 'blue' to the water to make the feathers look
whiter. I would also put Vaseline on their combs to brighten them. As
my sons grew up, it was David who was keen to go to the shows and

help me with the birds – Paul had no delight in poultry in those days! Then their interest reversed – Paul became interested but David thought it was a waste of money to keep buying hens and trying to improve the breed. He thought it would be better to buy good birds in the London show, and then show it in the local shows and win all the prizes. But when I had bought my first bird, that wasn't my bird – that was Mr. Binney's bird! There was no honour in that. I liked to see if I could improve the breed myself, and then when I won a class it was with my bird!

I am delighted that David's son Daniel and his daughter Rachel are now interested in showing.

I was showing poultry at the Gower Show just before the war, and continued until the show day moved from a Thursday to a Sunday. When I was young, no work was done on a Sunday – even the vegetables for our Sunday dinner had to be prepared the night before. As a Deacon of Tabernacle, I didn't feel it was right to have a show on a Sunday, so that was my last Gower show!

Included here amongst the young prize winners in the
poultry class are – back row, from left – 2nd left Alison Nicholas,
Hayley Thomas and Kelly Davies, and front row, from left –
Rhian Thomas, Phillip Tucker, Simon Tucker and Christian Powell.

HORTICULTURE

Leighton Evans of Three Crosses
who took first prize in the
mixed dahlia class.

Howard Thomas,
Garden Village, Kingsbridge,
with his prize-winning entries.

Inspecting the display are, from left – Ken Roberts, Bob Vicerage
and Emrys Collins.

CRAFTS

Catherine and Sarah Jones, of Lunnon Farm, with their prize-winning entries in the children's competitions in the craft tent. Their entries included a garland, a flower display, a painted stone and a puppet.
(By kind permission of Mrs. M. Jones).

PIGS

Esmor Owens with his prize-winning pig.

GOWER VINTAGE ENGINE SOCIETY

Robert Davies, Knelston, on his way to the show.
(By kind permission of John Harris, Penmaen).

Peter Sambrook and Scott Craig travelling to the show.
(By kind permission of John Harris, Penmaen).

THE GOWER VINTAGE ENGINE SOCIETY
REMEMBERED BY JOHN HARRIS, PENMAEN

The Gower Vintage Engine Society was formed in 1980 by a number of local enthusiasts who shared the same desire, which was to locate and then restore these fascinating items of agricultural nostalgia. Having first discovered and then painstakingly restored these engines to their former glory, it was felt that they should be shown to the public. What better place to show these beautifully renovated items of a bygone era than the Gower Show?

The first time we exhibited in the Gower Show was about 1980, and our site was located by the first copse on the left hand side of the road-way going down through the park. We used this spot for many years until the Show left Penrice for Swansea Airport. During this period our members grew in numbers and also the exhibits on show became more varied. We found that there were more tractors turning up, and we saw the engines driving various types of machinery – which was what they were made to do in the first place. The public really loved these so-called 'working exhibits'.

It was always an exciting time when we were preparing for the Show. Every engine and tractor would be cleaned and polished and made to look their best. Everything would be loaded onto trailers and taken to the Showground. The exhibits would be placed behind a secure fence – for safety reasons – they would be oiled and fuelled up and, with luck,

John Harris and some young enthusiasts
at the Gower Vintage Engine Society's display.
(By kind permission of John Harris, Penmaen).

they would run for the whole day. The tractor enthusiasts would also look forward to the Grand Parade around the main ring. This was always a favourite with spectators. At the end of the day, all exhibitors would receive a brass plaque which have the details of the Show engraved on it.

The Gower Show moved to Fairwood Airport and we all continued to support it, and put our vintage equipment on show for the public to enjoy. Fairwood Airport, although being level and with lots of hard standing, lacked any form of rural character. It was so wonderful to hear a few years ago that the Gower Show would be returning to Penrice Castle.

The Gower Vintage Engine Society wound up about this time, but we are still to be found showing off our engines and tractors – on an individual basis this time. The vintage stand now includes classic cars and in the centennial year we even had a London Transport Routemaster bus.

It is great to be back in Penrice Castle grounds – the perfect setting for an agricultural show, and to be part of the Centenary Gower Show was something special.

FOUNDER MEMBERS OF THE GOWER VINTAGE ENGINE SOCIETY
From left – Ron Parry, Ossie Jones, Adrian Richards, Robert Davies,
Peter Sambrook and John Harris.
(By kind permission of Robert Davies).

HORSES

Beverley Pritchard, Cae Ivor Farm, Llanrhidian, being presented with the Championship Cup for her prize-winning 'Saline of Drum' by Mr. A. Turnbull. John Pritchard, Show Director, is to his right.
(By kind permission of Miss B. Pritchard).

Carey Knox with her daughter Corrine and pony 'Evendale Charisma', a competitor in the 1986 Gower Show. The pony went on to win the Horse of the Year Show in Olympia.
(By kind permission of Mrs. C. Knox).

Emma Bladen on 'Crystal'.
(By kind permission of Mrs. E. Beynon).

Dawn Bowen showing 'Cae Mansel Melody'.
(By kind permission of Mrs. F. Bowen).

GOWER SHOW, 1994
2nd left – Mr Anthony Oliver Watkins (Australia), Ellis Davies (Chairman),
and Tudor Jones (Towyn, North Wales), with the overall Champion
'Caerberllan Heather'.
(By kind permission of A. Ellis Davies).

Mrs. Gwyneth Jones, Lunnon, with Christopher Ball.
(By kind permission of John Furneaux).

Corrine Knox competing in the 1995 Gower Show with her pony 'Thomas'.
(By kind permission of Mrs. C. Knox).

Alison Evans, Scurlage, competing in the show jumping
in the 1995 Gower Show on 'Trixie'.
(By kind permission of Alison Evans).

David Evans, Penclawdd.

Neil Pritchard, Cae Ivor Farm.

Natalie Dark, Llanrhidian, riding 'Login Black Magic'.
(By kind permission of Natalie Dark).

Martyn Jenkins.

Alison Thomas driving a tandem owned by Lt. Col. Rosser John.

Hungarian Csikos Riders who were special guests
at the 1990 Gower Show.

Csikos rider in action.

SHEEP

A sheep shearing demonstration by Nicky Beynon.

Rob Howell, aged 8, of Manselfield Farm, Murton,
with his prize-winning Ryeland.

Dewi Evans with his two Suffolk ewes.

'Any other breed ram class', with, from right – Keith Evans, Scurlage Castle,
Kay Beynon, Jeff Griffiths, Llanrhidian, Rowland Pritchard, Weobley,
Huw Phillips, Colin Williams, Mark Davies and Ken Elliot.
(By kind permission of Keith Evans, Scurlage Castle).

Keith Evans with his 1st prize-winning ram.
In the background is Mr. Evans, Chirk, class judge.
(By kind permission of Keith Evans, Scurlage Castle).

SHEEPDOG TRIALS

Eirwen Davies with his dog.

GOATS

'Any other variety goats'. Included here are – Helen Foster, Gill Wharmbey, Jean Macleod, Kristie Foster, Ruby Parfitt, Dave Wharmbey and Maureen Parton.

From left – Judge Graham Godfrey, Adeline Shackles and Lorna Frame.
(By kind permission of Mrs. K. Frame).

THE GOAT SECTION
AT FAIRWOOD

REMEMBERED BY MRS. KATH FRAME

I took over the goat section from Mrs. Brook in 1988. The day before the Show, as soon as the tent was up, work would begin on erecting the hurdles. This was done with great pride by Mr. John Grove. Anita Grove and I would then label the pens and lay fresh straw in each pen. We then took delivery of a kitchen stove and a hot water boiler – the goats only drank warm water!

Later in the day, the exhibitors began to arrive – they came from as far away as London, The Midlands, Yorkshire, and many areas of Wales. As there were only 30 judges covering the whole of the British Isles, they also came from far and wide. The exhibitors bedded the goats down and then got themselves organised and ready for the day ahead. At 6 p.m. they milked the goats and then had supper.

With the help of my daughters Lorna and Madeline, we would prepare enough food for approximately 30 exhibitors. We would cook beef and chicken casseroles and make trifles and fruit pies. We then cleared up and took home a boot full of dirty dishes. Great fun! We would return the next morning with a full English breakfast. Many of the exhibitors would have had a restless night as some of them slept in the tent with the goats. Judging went on for most of the day, as there were seven classes – each split into Milkers, Goatlings and Kids. All these were put into date of birth order.

After judging, winners were presented with their appropriate cups – then the task of clearing up began. The following day, John Grove and I would stack the hurdles ready to be collected by Rowland Pritchard.

Through the succeeding years, less people were keeping milking goats, so entries began to fall. At this time it became necessary for each exhibit to be tested for Caprine Arthritic Encephalitis incurring hefty vets bills, and with increasing restrictions on the sale of goat's milk, it became difficult to find buyers for it, so subsequently fewer people were keeping goats. In order not to lose the goat section we began to exhibit Pygmy Goats and in 1998 we had 30 entries. These were a great attraction – especially to the children.

Eventually the cost of tentage and judges' expenses became too much, and, sadly, 2001 saw the end of the goat section in the Gower Show.

THE CROP GROWING COMPETITION, 1996

Several weeks before the Gower Show, farmers who had entered the crop growing competition would have their fields visited by the judge. The winner would be announced on the day of the Show.

Messrs. William and Albert Parry, Moor Corner Farm,
with the judge, Mr. Lucas.
(By kind permission of John Furneaux).

Derek Hanks (judge) with John Tucker, The Beeches, Horton.
(By kind permission of John Furneaux).

Rowland Pritchard, Weobley Castle, with judge, Derek Hanks.
(By kind permission of John Furneaux).

Viv Jones, Lunnon, with judge, Derek Hanks.
(By kind permission of John Furneaux).

THE YOUNG FARMERS

Clare Bevan and Lisa Hopkins of Gower Young Farmers watch as a contestant takes part in a 'Guess the weight of a sheep' competition. The Texel ram was part of Keith Evans' flock, Scurlage Castle.

Chris Mabbett and Anthony Griffiths lifting hay bales.

WOMEN'S INSTITUTE

Daphne Furneaux and Jane Davies with Llandewi & Knelston's winning entry in the W.I.'s co-operative section.

GOWER SHOW, 1995
Hazel Williams, a Gower Show collector for 40 years, is presented with a
gold watch in recognition of her service, by Howard Morgan.
(By kind permission of Mrs. Hazel Williams).

Pat Williams and Joyce Ellis, judges in the unaffiliated show jumping,
watching events in the main ring in the 1994 Gower Show.
(By kind permission of Pat Williams).

A centennial celebration for The National Trust, 1995.
From left – Pauline Bevan, Secretary, Councillor Howard Morgan,
President of the Gower Show, and Sian Musgrave, Warden.
(By kind permission of The National Trust).

GOWER GROWERS WALES LTD.
Andrew Oliver, manager of Gower Growers Wales Ltd.,
based at Little Reynoldston Farm, pictured in the National Union
of Farmers' tent with some produce, which was sold to raise
money for Arthritis and Rheumatism research.
(By kind permission of Andrew Oliver).

Edna and Dick Beynon, Llanrhidian.
(By kind permission of Mrs. E. Beynon).

A RAINY DAY AT THE SHOW

The 1997 Gower Show at Fairwood was described in the *South Wales Evening Post* as: 'a washout, as cold winds and pouring rain drove the usual crowds away.' The number of people visiting the show was the lowest for more than 10 years, and the gate receipts were down by more than 75%.

The organisers said that all entries were up on last year and only one exhibitor had cancelled – a sun care and sun cream stall!

But mostly there was 'sunshine and bumper crowds'.

CHAPTER 5

Back Home

South Wales Evening Post, August 2002 –

TOP SHOW RETURNING TO HOME

'The Gower Show is returning to its traditional home at Penrice this year. After a dozen years at Swansea Airport, South West Wales' biggest one-day agricultural show is moving back to its old venue overlooking Oxwich Bay courtesy of the Methuen-Campbell family.'

PREPARING FOR THE CENTENNIAL SHOW, 2005

'Base camp'.
The centre of operations – John Furneaux's office.
(By kind permission of Daphne Furneaux).

Helen Davies cutting the grass in readiness for the Mitsubishi trade stand.
(By kind permission of Daphne Furneaux).

Gower Young Farmers assist show director, John Furneaux,
to erect the cattle pens.
From left – James Furneaux, Keith Evans, Phil Grove, Daniel Tucker,
John Furneaux and Sian Tucker.
(By kind permission of Daphne Furneaux).

SHOW DAY, 2005

'A country show again, in its usual domain'.
(By kind permission of Stephen Thomas).

Dai Jones, Llanilar, judging the cattle in the 2005 Gower Show.
(By kind permission of Mrs. Enid Hughes).

James Roderick, Scurlage, in the Young Handler class.
(By kind permission of Mrs. Enid Hughes).

Louise Furneaux, Alistair Ross and Caitlin Furneaux-Ross.
(By kind permission of Daphne Furneaux).

Harry Heather with the alpacas.
(With Harry's kind permission).

From left – Gill Balsdon, Martyn Jenkins and Carey Knox.
All have served as secretary of the Gower Show.
(By kind permission of Mrs. Carey Knox).

150

Line up for the judging of the Championship bull.
(By kind permission of Stephen Thomas).

Elizabeth Roderick with 'Brangwyn 1 Pathfinder'.
(By kind permission of Stephen Thomas).

Martyn Jenkins
with 'Meiros Ronaldo'.
(By kind permission of Stephen Thomas).

Mark Davies, Gelli Onnen,
with his daughter, Bethan.
(By kind permission of Stephen Thomas).

Richard and William Tucker.
(By kind permission of Stephen Thomas).

Line up for judging.
(By kind permission of Stephen Thomas).

Ivan Lloyd, Vet. Surgeon.
(By kind permission of Stephen Thomas).

Russell Howell.
(By kind permission of Stephen Thomas).

Dilys and Gordon Griffiths
with Tony Jones.

Tom Williams.
'Tom the Box.'

'It was a great day out, for locals there's no doubt,
A chance to meet and talk with friends and neighbours.'

John Beynon, Gower poet.

(Photographs by kind permission of Stephen Thomas, Tal-y-Ffrawe).

John Davies, Gelli Groes.

Howard Grove, New Henllys,
and Eirwen Harry, East Pilton.

David Prosser, centre,
with R. Mabbett Hennyswell.

Vivian Tucker, Knelston Hall,
and Mark Davies.

(Photographs by kind permission of Stephen Thomas, Tal-y-Ffrawe).

John Gilchrist, Morgan Stores.

Heulwen Griffiths, Fairwood Corner,
Jeff Griffiths, Llanrhidian,
with Chris and Mary Farmer.

(Photographs by kind permission of Stephen Thomas, Tal-y-Ffrawe).

Gower Show Secretary, Emily Gordon.

Aubrey Oliver, Judge of the Supreme Champion of the Horse and Pony classes,
with Dick Beynon, President Elect.
(By kind permission of Aubrey Oliver).

When the show was over, an evening barbeque was held for the work
team.

From left – John Furneaux, Show Director, Rowland Pritchard, Chairman,
and Richard Gordon.
(By kind permission of Daphne Furneaux).

Relaxing at the barbeque are – from left – Edward Harris, John Furneaux,
Thomas Methuen-Campbell, Ruth and Malcolm Ridge.
(By kind permission of Daphne Furneaux).

The following morning, Gower Young Farmers acted as litter pickers,
returning the beautiful Penrice Park to its natural splendour.

Sarah and Catherine Jones, two Gower Young Farmers,
take a well-earned rest from their litter picking.
(By kind permission of Daphne Furneaux).

CHAPTER 6

Gower Show Officials

PRESIDENT OF THE GOWER SHOW

Throughout the hundred years of the Gower Show, the show has had sixteen Presidents. The first president in 1906 was Admiral Sir Algernon Lyons G.C.B. who was succeeded in 1909 by his wife Lady Lyons. Miss Emily Talbot in turn succeeded her. Lord Blythswood later became President, his wife Lady Evelyn Blythswood taking on the position after his death in 1930.

Lady Blythswood remained President for 28 years, until her death in 1958. Her grandson Christopher Methuen-Campbell succeeded her; when the Show moved to Fairwood in 1987, it was decided that a new President would be chosen – each to serve for two years.

> 1987 and 1988 – A. B. Turnbull.
> 1989 and 1990 – Ernest Richards.
> 1991 and 1992 – Morgan Jones.
> 1993 and 1994 – Ernest Jones.
> 1995 and 1996 – Councillor H. Morgan, J.P.
> 1997 and 1998 – D. Methuen-Campbell.
> 1999 and 2000 – E. G. Griffiths.
> 2001 – C. J. Beynon was the president,
>   but because of the foot and mouth epidemic,
>   no show was held.
> 2002 and 2003 – C. J. Beynon.
> 2004 and 2005 – J. Tucker.

The President in 2006 is Dick Beynon, Llanrhidian.

PRESIDENT AND OFFICIALS OF THE GOWER SHOW

From left – Emily Gordon, Keith Lewis, Paul Tucker, Peter Muxworthy, Ellis Davies, John Tucker (President), John Furneaux, Dick Beynon, Ernest Smith, Rowland Pritchard, Gordon Griffiths.

SECRETARY

The first secretary of the show, Mr. Arthur Anthony, held the position for 45 years. After his death in 1951, two secretaries were appointed – Mr. P. G. Davies, and Mr. R. W. H. Jenkins of Kilvrough Farm shared the responsibility. Mr. Rowland Jenkins was succeeded by his son, Martin Jenkins.

Mrs. Gill Balsdon became secretary in 1976, and on her retirement in 1993, Mrs. Carey Knox took over the position. Mrs. Knox, as the daughter of Mr. Rowland Jenkins, was continuing the family involvement in the Gower Show.

The present secretary is Miss Emily Gordon.

TREASURER

The Gower Show has had two long-term treasurers; in the early years Mr. C. C. Vivian, of the Midland Bank, held the position, and since 1987 Peter Muxworthy has been the Society's treasurer.

Mrs. J. Methuen-Campbell (centre left), who, with her son,
Thomas Methuen-Campbell, hosts the Gower Show at Penrice Park.
She is photographed here with officials and vice-presidents of the Gower Show.
From left – Christopher Beynon, Howard Morgan, Peter Muxworthy,
Thomas Methuen-Campbell, Mrs. J. Methuen-Campbell,
John Tucker (President), Ellis Davies, Hazel Williams, Tony Jones, Dick Beynon,
Gwyn Griffiths, John Furneaux, Martyn Jenkins and Gordon Griffiths.

CHAIRMAN

Few records survive of the Gower Show officials in the early years – the earliest programme available records that in 1926 R. A. Jeffreys was the chairman. In 1930, Glyn James held the position, as did Arthur Griffiths in 1932. In 1936, W. Kneath was recorded as chairman, and from 1939 onwards, the chairman is recorded in the minute book of the Gower Agricultural Society.

1939.   S. Richards J.P,. Rhossili

No show was held during the war years

1946.   C. B. Layton
1947.   Gwyn Beynon
1948.   Col. F. S. Morgan
1949.   Ernest Stevens
1950.   Gwilym Pugh
1951.   Ernest Richards
1952.   William Jones
1953.   G. E. Lewis
1954.   G. S. Eaton
1955.   Richard James
1956.   T. Jones
1957.   George Richards
1958.   B. R. Beynon
1959.   Glyn Jeffreys
1960.   F. J. Taylor
1961.   W. T. Williams
1962.   Glyn A. Hughes
1963.   Norman Richards
1964.   Ernest Jones
1965.   B. J. James
1966.   L. J. Jeffreys
1967.   John S. Pritchard
1968.   Glyn Beynon

1969.	T. Morgan Jones
1970.	Henry Beynon
1971.	Milwyn Layton
1972.	C. G. Grove
1973.	Glyn Rogers
1974.	A. H. L. Eccles
1975.	D. J. Davies
1976.	Martyn Jenkins
1977.	T. Beynon
1978.	John Tucker
1979.	Les March
1980.	Ernest Smith
1981.	William Gambold
1982.	Terry Thomas
1983.	Fred Richards
1984.	Gordon Griffiths
1985.	Robert James
1986/7	John Furneaux
1988/9	Paul Tucker
1990/1	Dick Beynon
1992/3	A. Jones
1994/5	Ellis Davies
1996/7	John Beynon
1998/9	Leighton Pritchard
2000/2	Gordon Mitchell

No show was held in 2001

2003/4	Mrs. K. Frame
2005/6	R. Pritchard

SHOW DIRECTOR

The Show Director from 1906 until 1939 was Hopkin Llewellyn Prichard, the agent of the Penrice Estate. Major Smartt served as Director from 1946 until 1950, when Mr. Alan Turnbull took over the role.

Mr. John Pritchard of Weobley Castle succeeded him. John Pritchard died in 1989, and the Gower Agricultural Society recognised his contribution to the Society by establishing 'The John Pritchard Memorial Bursary' which was intended to further the agricultural education of students from the parishes of Gower.

John Furneaux has been Director of the Gower Show since 1989.

JOHN FURNEAUX, SHOW DIRECTOR

Show Director of the Gower Show is a great honour and privilege, and my predecessors have all given great service to the Show.

The Gower Show has been part of my life since moving to Gower in 1972, working for the then Show Director Mr. Alan Turnbull. Cattle were allowed back to the show after a long absence due to an outbreak of Brucellosis at the Home Farm. The lack of cattle entries led to the orders, 'ANY CATTLE THAT WILL LEAD ON A HALTER TAKE TO THE SHOW!'

A few years later when Daphne and I moved to Burry, our job involved helping her grandfather Peter Jones and Harry Pugh set up and

164

clear away the show. The job would last about four weeks, and upon their retirement we took over the job as a family. My son Richard would drive an old M.F. 65 with limited brakes, and we all helped to clear up the rubbish. The show would be put up in a week and taken down in three days. Today we start on the Wednesday before show day, and have it erected by Saturday night and cleared away (90%) by Monday night.

A work move to Great Pitton Farm meant the end of working for the show, but in 1986 I was elected chairman, a position I held for two years – the last show of the Penrice era and the first show at Fairwood Airport. Two years later, with the very sad death of John Pritchard, a man who had given the show so much and who had been a great inspiration to me, I was appointed Show Director.

Swansea Airport as a show site had many limitations, and one great advantage – tarmac on which to park cars. No more towing in and out! However the grass areas had some very wet spots, so towing vehicles never ceased. Lack of an adequate water supply had to be addressed to allow the toilets to function; it was always seen as an indication as the size of the crowd as to how the toilets functioned. Problems meant good crowd – no problems small crowd!

During the fourteen years that the show was held at the airport, the finances of the society declined, marquee hire rose out of all proportion, and gate receipts were in decline, the site lacked character and was out of favour with many Gower people, but who was to know what awaited around the corner? Air Wales was to start flying commercially which meant that all other activities would have to cease at the airport. Then Foot and Mouth struck! No show in 2001. Time to look to the future of the show.

With great support from Mr. Christopher Beynon and the willingness of Mrs. Judith Methuen-Campbell and Thomas Methuen-Campbell, the show returned to Penrice. I will never forget the night that Christopher and I met the Methuen-Campbell's to be told that not only would the show be welcome back in Penrice, but also that the only place it should be was in the park. The Gower Show was back home!

During this uncertain time, I would also like to recall the Society's thanks to Rowland Pritchard who was willing to make land available for the 2002 show, if no permanent site had been found.

The 2002 Gower Show back in Penrice – Foot and Mouth under control, but heavy restrictions on the movement of farm animals and show sites. The committee decided that the show would return as a full show with all animal classes available. A great deal of work and form-filling by Miss Emily Gordon our secretary, and a satisfactory D.E.F.R.A. inspection (by officials who do not like television cameras), hailed the return of the animal classes. The goat section decided to disband which was a great pity. Show Day 2002 was something special – full livestock classes and what would turn out to be a record attendance. The car parks were full – but more space was found with grateful thanks to Simon Bevan, the Penrice Farm manager. This was the year that they were to make the television series 'Summer in Gower'. The Gower Show was to feature, and television crews like it when things don't go as planned. It was not my finest moment with cars waiting to get in, queues building, and a film crew following me around. Unfortunately, whilst trying to contact Rowland on my mobile phone, the sound crew picked me up saying ' If Rowland's there – wake him up!' I think Rowland has forgiven me – but it's still worth a pint! The end of the day would see the finances back in the black, and a show director's life is a lot easier with a healthy bank balance!

Three more excellent shows have followed and it's a tribute to all the unpaid volunteers who make the day flow, and ensure the smooth running of the show. They all contribute to the brilliant day it has become, as do all our Sponsors who give so generously, and the people of Gower who have raised membership to new heights.

Being a Show Director of the Gower Show is a great feeling. I enjoy hitting posts in, and laying water pipes before the show, and then seeing all the hard work culminate in a great day. From meeting old friends to clearing up the rubbish on Monday morning – and all the time having the support of my fellow directors and committee.

One hundred years gone – here's to the next one hundred years!

Acknowledgements

The Gower Agricultural Society would like to thank Martin L. Williams, Llanrhidian, who has made a significant contribution to this book by enhancing and compiling all the photographs and documents provided.

Unless otherwise acknowledged, all photographs are by courtesy of the *South Wales Evening Post*. The Gower Agricultural Society would like to thank Mr. Seeney, Editor of the *South Wales Evening Post*, for allowing these photographs to be used in this publication.

Also . . .

> Dick Beynon
> Richard Brighton, Cambrian Index
> Ellis Davies
> Daphne Furneaux
> Mrs. Marilyn Jones, Local Studies Librarian,
>   and the helpful staff of Swansea Reference Library.
> Emyr Nicholas, Eddie John and the staff of Dinefwr Press
>   for their friendly and professional advice and assistance.
> Mike Phelps, Glamorgan Archive Service.
> Stephen Thomas.
> Nigel Williams.

*

Our very grateful thanks to Mrs. Pat Williams for all the work she has done in researching and compiling this book, her efforts are so gratefully appreciated by all the committee of The Gower Agricultural Society. Without her commitment, this book would not have been produced.

Bibliography

The Centenary of the Gower Agricultural Society, Thomas Methuen-Campbell.
A History of the Gower Show, David R. Gwynn.
Gower Church magazines.
The South Wales Daily Post.
The South Wales Evening Post.
The Herald of Wales.
Service with a Smile, Ann Roberts.